CLIMATE FINANCE LANDSCAPE OF ASIA AND THE PACIFIC

AUGUST 2023

ASIAN DEVELOPMENT BANK

ADB

Contents

Tables, Figures, and Boxes iv

Foreword vi

Acknowledgments viii

Abbreviations ix

Executive Summary xi

1   Background 1

2   Methods and Approaches 3

3   Climate Finance Landscape of Asia and the Pacific 8

   3.1   Sources and Intermediaries 9

   3.2   Sectors 13

   3.3   Geographic Flows 16

   3.4   Financial Instruments 17

   3.5   Challenges and Opportunities in Mobilizing Climate Finance in Asia and the Pacific 18

4   Subregional Landscape Assessment 26

   4.1   Central and West Asia 26

   4.2   East Asia 34

   4.3   South Asia 42

   4.4   Southeast Asia 53

   4.5   Pacific 66

Appendix 78

References 86

Tables, Figures, and Boxes

TABLES

1	Subregional Groupings of ADB Developing Countries in Asia and the Pacific	6
2	Multilateral Funds Supporting Asia and the Pacific	11
3	Snapshot of Climate Change Priorities in Central and West Asia, 2018–2019	27
4	Snapshot of Climate Change Priorities in East Asia, 2018–2019	36
5	Snapshot of Climate Change Priorities in South Asia, 2018–2019	43
6	Snapshot of Climate Change Priorities in Southeast Asia, 2018–2019	54
7	Indonesia Climate Mitigation Investment Needs (Total 2020–2030), Based on Updated NDC	62
8	Public International Climate Finance Access and Mobilization in Indonesia	64
9	Snapshot of Climate Change Priorities in the Pacific, 2018–2019	68
10	Environment and Climate Adaptation Levy (ECAL) in Fiji—Coverage and Rates, 2018–2019	76
A1	Asia and the Pacific Climate Finance, 2018–2019, by Sector and Subsector	78
A2	Asia and the Pacific Climate Finance, 2018–2019, by Recipient Subregion and Country	79
A3	Asia and the Pacific Climate Finance, 2018–2019, by Financing Source	81
A4	Asia and the Pacific Climate Finance, 2018–2019, by Financing Instrument	82
A5	Asia and the Pacific Climate Finance Needs up to 2030	82
A6	Climate Finance by Development Finance Institution	85

FIGURES

1	Total Climate Finance Flows to Asia and the Pacific, 2018–2019	xv
2	Steps in Assessing the Climate Finance Landscape in Asia and the Pacific	3
3	Snapshot of Climate Finance Flows in Asia and the Pacific, 2018–2019	5
5	Climate Finance in Asia and the Pacific, by Subregion, 2018–2019	8
6	Climate Finance in Asia and the Pacific, by Subregion and Sector, 2018–2019	9
7	Public Sources and Intermediaries of Climate Finance in Asia and the Pacific, 2018–2019	10
8	Private Sources and Intermediaries of Climate Finance in Asia and the Pacific, 2018–2019	12
9	Mitigation, Adaptation, and Dual-Benefit Finance in Asia and the Pacific, 2018–2019	13
10	Total Mitigation Finance in Asia and the Pacific, 2018–2019	14
11	Total Adaptation Finance in Asia and the Pacific, 2018–2019	16
11	Destination Subregions of Climate Finance in Asia and the Pacific, 2018–2019	17

11 Breakdown of Financial Instruments for Climate Finance in Asia and the Pacific, 2018–2019   18
12 Mitigation, Adaptation, and Dual-Benefit Finance in Central and West Asia, 2018–2019   30
13 Breakdown of Climate Finance Instruments in Central and West Asia, 2018–2019   31
14 Mitigation, Adaptation, and Dual-Benefit Finance in East Asia, 2018–2019   38
15 Breakdown of Climate Finance Instruments in East Asia, 2018–2019   38
16 Mitigation, Adaptation, and Dual-Benefit Finance in South Asia, 2018–2019   47
17 Breakdown of Climate Finance Instruments in South Asia, 2018–2019   47
18 Climate Investment Potential vs. Current Investment Level in South Asia, 2018–2019   48
19 Evolution of the Climate Financing Framework in Bangladesh   50
20 Tracked Climate Finance, 2018–2019, and Estimated Annual Climate Finance Needs   53
    in Bangladesh, 2021–2030
21 Mitigation, Adaptation, and Dual-Benefit Finance in Southeast Asia, 2018– 2019   57
22 Breakdown of Climate Finance Instruments in Southeast Asia, 2018–2019   58
23 Infrastructure Investment Needs in Indonesia, 2020–2040   62
24 Mitigation and Adaptation Finance in the Pacific Subregion, 2018–2019   73
25 Breakdown of Climate Finance Instruments in the Pacific, 2018–2019   74

BOXES

1 Data Limitations and Gaps in Climate Finance Tracking for 38 Developing Countries in 2018–2019   7
2 Narrowing the Data Gap—Efforts to Track Private Investment and Domestic National   25
   Climate Finance in Asia and the Pacific
3 Climate Finance Centre as Climate Finance Coordinator Responsible for MRV Mechanism   34
   in the Kyrgyz Republic
4 Mongolian Green Taxonomy—A "Best Practice" in Climate Finance Transparency   42
5 Climate Finance Tracking Methodology in Bangladesh   51
6 Strengthening Indonesia's Climate Finance Ecosystem through Climate Budget Tagging   65
   and Country Platforms to Improve Climate Finance Tracking
7 Fiji's Subregional Learning and Sharing as an Effort to Close the Knowledge and   77
   Capacity Gap in the Pacific for Climate Finance Readiness

Foreword

The Asia and Pacific region is a crucial part of global efforts to curb climate change. It contributes around 50% of the global greenhouse gas emission (GHG) total, and many countries in the region are vulnerable to the adverse impact of climate change. These countries include several small island developing states and 11 of the 20 countries most affected by extreme weather events in 2000–2019 (Germanwatch e. V. 2021).

All developing countries of the Asian Development Bank (ADB) in the region have prepared their Nationally Determined Contributions (NDCs) and are at different stages in the preparation of their long-term strategies (LTSs) for low-emission and climate-resilient development, laying out their commitments toward achieving the goals of the Paris Agreement. These mitigation, adaptation, and other climate measures committed to by governments need financing in order to be realized. However, according to the Climate Policy Initiative (2021), current global investments fall short and annual climate finance must increase by 590% to meet the climate objectives set for 2030.

In Asia and the Pacific, a region where swift and massive climate action is necessary, governments, financing institutions, the private sector, and key stakeholders must work together to mobilize sufficient and timely climate finance to support such action. Besides exploring additional financing sources and making these sources available for climate action, all these players must examine the effectiveness of the current use of climate finance, and the first step in that direction would be to assess how climate finance flows from the sources to the recipients.

This publication assesses the climate finance landscape of Asia and the Pacific, and of each of the five subregions that compose it: Central and West Asia, East Asia, South Asia, Southeast Asia, and the Pacific. It traces climate finance flows—from the sources (e.g., public, private) to the financing instruments employed (e.g., loans, grants) and the uses of funds (e.g., adaptation, mitigation, sectors)—and seeks to reveal the gaps in climate finance so that these can be addressed.

Climate Finance Landscape of Asia and the Pacific is intended for sources, intermediaries, and recipients of climate finance—including governments in developing economies and developed countries, development finance institutions, the private sector, and civil society stakeholders, who can make climate finance available and accessible, and channel it to the countries, institutions, and sectors that need it most.

In 2021, ADB announced its ambition to increase its cumulative climate financing to $100 billion between 2019 and 2030, and to allocate $34 billion of this amount for cumulative adaptation and resilience investments, and $66 billion for cumulative mitigation financing. ADB also aspires to reach $12 billion in cumulative climate finance for private sector operations by 2030, and to crowd in an additional $18–$30 billion to support the development of more commercially viable and climate-friendly businesses. Guided by *Climate Finance Landscape of Asia and the Pacific*, ADB—as the "climate bank" of the region—can strategically direct resources to support the low-carbon and climate-resilient development objectives of sovereign and nonsovereign clients. In 2022, ADB committed climate financing from own resources reached $6.7 billion, of which $2.7 billion is on adaptation and resilience and $4.0 billion is on mitigation.

With this publication, ADB hopes to enhance collective knowledge of climate finance and help mobilize financing for the effective design and implementation of climate actions to achieve the global goals set in the Paris Agreement.

Noelle O'Brien
Director, Climate Change
Climate Change and Sustainable Development Department
Asian Development Bank

Acknowledgments

This publication is a knowledge product of the Asian Development Bank (ADB) under the regional knowledge and support technical assistance program Building Institutional Capacity: Delivering Solutions under Operational Priority 3 of Strategy 2030 (TA 6627-REG)—Study on the Climate Finance Landscape of Asia and the Pacific (54176-001).

It is based on the implementing consultant's report prepared by the Climate Policy Initiative's Luthfyana Larasati, Tiza Mafira, Pedro Fernandes, Baysa Naran, Rajashree Padmanabi, Chavi Meattle, and Muhammad Zeki.

The report was prepared under the overall guidance of Esmyra Javier, climate change specialist (climate finance), Climate Change, Resilience and Environment Cluster, Climate Change and Sustainable Development Department (CCSD), with support from Hannah Ebro (former consultant) and Marlene Vinluan, senior analyst and project coordinator.

The report benefited significantly from the comments and valuable insights by Jiro Tominaga, country director; Srinivasan Ancha, principal climate change specialist; Benita Ainabe, senior financial sector specialist of the Southeast Asia Department (SERD); Jeff Bowyer, senior climate change specialist of the Pacific Department (PARD); Dongmei Guo, environment specialist of the East Asia Department (EARD); Belinda Hewitt, senior disaster risk management specialist of SDCC (formerly from EARD); Nathan Rive, senior climate change specialist; Malte Maass, climate change specialist; Kathleen Coballes, climate change officer of the Central and West Asia Department (CWRD), Eleonora Windisch, advisor and head (Portfolio, Results and Quality Control Unit); Kyla May Matias, associate climate change officer of South Asia Department (SARD); Saranga Gajasinghe, safeguards officer; Utsav Kumar, principal country economist of Sri Lanka Resident Mission; and SARD consultants Bobbie Gerpacio and Rosa Perez.

The manuscript was copyedited by Mary Ann Asico and proofread by Mary Martha Merilo; and Ross Locsin Laccay took charge of the design and layout.

Abbreviations

ADB	Asian Development Bank
AFOLU	agriculture, forestry, and other land use
ASEAN	Association of Southeast Asian Nations
BAU	business as usual
BPDLH	Badan Pengelola Dana Lingkungan Hidup (Indonesian Environment Fund)
CBT	climate budget tagging
CFC	Climate Finance Center, Kyrgyz Republic
CFF	Climate Fiscal Framework
CPI	Climate Policy Initiative
DFI	development finance institution
DRM	disaster risk management
ECAL	Environment and Climate Adaptation Levy, Fiji
GCF	Green Climate Fund
GDP	gross domestic product
GEF	Global Environment Facility
GHG	greenhouse gas
$GtCO_2e$	gigatonnes (billion metric tons) of carbon dioxide equivalent
ICCTF	Indonesia Climate Change Trust Fund
IFC	International Finance Corporation
IPCC	Intergovernmental Panel on Climate Change
Lao PDR	Lao People's Democratic Republic
LTS	long-term strategy
MDB	multilateral development bank
MRV	measurement, reporting, and verification
NDC	Nationally Determined Contribution
NIE	national implementing entity
NZE	net-zero emissions
PNG	Papua New Guinea
PRC	People's Republic of China

PV	photovoltaic
SDG	Sustainable Development Goal
SOE	state-owned enterprise
TA	technical assistance
tCO_2e	tonnes (metric tons) of carbon dioxide equivalent
UNEP	United Nations Environment Programme
UNFCCC	The United Nations Framework Convention on Climate Change
WECOOP	European Union–Central Asia Environment, Climate Change and Water Cooperation Program

Executive Summary

Climate change is a major concern for Asia and the Pacific. This region, where developing countries most vulnerable to the impact of climate change are located, is the biggest contributor to greenhouse gas (GHG) emissions: it is responsible for over half of global emissions.

Various efforts and measures have been taken at the national, regional, and global levels by Asia and Pacific countries in response to climate change impact, as shown in their Nationally Determined Contributions (NDCs) and their participation in the United Nations Framework Convention on Climate Change (UNFCCC) and the Paris Agreement. Some countries recently updated their NDCs to reflect more ambitious climate targets. Developing countries also conveyed the message that those targets would not be achieved through their own efforts alone, and that they would need international assistance to mobilize and scale up finance toward low-carbon transition and climate-resilient development.

Given the urgency of meeting the goals of the Paris Agreement, this report seeks to enhance the knowledge base, and to support the developing countries of the Asian Development Bank (ADB) in expanding climate change action, through a quantitative and qualitative assessment of the climate finance landscape of Asia and the Pacific, as well as in-depth regional analyses of its five subregions: Central and West Asia, East Asia, South Asia, Southeast Asia, and the Pacific. The report uses data from 2018–2019 and includes an overview of the impact of the coronavirus disease (COVID-19) pandemic on finance flows in 2020, based on the Climate Policy Initiative's Global Landscape of Climate Finance (CPI 2019a, 2020, 2021) and national tracking initiatives such as India's Landscape of Green Finance, Indonesia's Landscape of Private Climate Finance, and the Landscape of Climate Finance of the People's Republic of China (PRC).

The report has the following sections:
- **Section 1: Background and context** on the importance of understanding climate finance flows in Asia and the Pacific, particularly in relation to the Paris Agreement.
- **Section 2: Methods and approaches** used in assessing the climate finance landscape of Asia and the Pacific, covering mitigation, adaptation, and dual-benefit financing. The assessment is based on 2018–2019 data from the CPI's Global Landscape of Climate Finance (CPI 2019a), including sources of climate finance and types of recipients.
- **Section 3: Climate finance landscape of Asia and the Pacific**, which contains an assessment of financing according to source (public vs. private), uses and sectors (mitigation vs. adaptation), instruments (debt vs. equity), and geographic flow (final destination of climate finance), as well as a discussion on key challenges and opportunities in mobilizing climate finance in Asia and the Pacific.
- **Section 4: Climate finance landscape of the five subregions of Asia and the Pacific**. A subsection for each subregion (i) describes and gives an overview of the subregional context; (ii) assesses the climate finance landscape and key financing highlights and features; (iii) identifies challenges and opportunities to narrow the finance gap, which could lead to scaled-up financing; and (iv) highlights practices and lessons learned in managing climate finance, through case studies on selected countries.

Climate Finance Landscape of Asia and the Pacific

In 2018–2019, Asia and the Pacific spent $519.9 billion in climate finance—$225.6 billion in 2018 and $294.3 billion in 2019 (30% more than in 2018). The public sector contributed the most to total climate finance flows, at $351.8 billion (68%); of this amount, $241.7 billion came from development finance institutions (DFIs), the top public sector contributors. Public finance was the main source of climate finance for most subregions in Asia and the Pacific, except South Asia, which relied almost equally on private finance. The private sector's 32% contribution ($168.1 billion) to total flows during the period derived mainly from corporations, household spending, and commercial financial institutions.

Commitments, in both the public and private sectors, were made mostly in the energy sector. The public sector focused on accelerating a low-carbon energy transition; the private sector, on the financial attractiveness of energy production and distribution due to its more mature technology, bankable project size, and available risk mitigation schemes.

Mitigation finance, particularly in the energy sector, dominated climate finance in Asia and the Pacific in 2018–2019. It reached $472.5 billion (91% of total flows), driven by finance directed for the most part toward solar photovoltaic (PV), wind, and hydropower generation in the PRC and India. Financing for low-carbon transport also grew rapidly, as more rail and transit investments were made by corporations and public sector stakeholders, and electric vehicles gained wider use among households (CPI 2019a).

Adaptation finance accounted for 8% of total flows ($40.8 billion), and dual-benefit finance, for projects with both mitigation and adaptation outcomes, for the remaining 1% ($6.7 billion). Adaptation finance rose by 31% during the 2018–2019 period, fr om $17.7 billion to $23.1 billion, signaling efforts to achieve a better balance between mitigation and adaptation finance, in response to Article 9 of the Paris Agreement. But a wide disparity remained between the estimated costs of adaptation and the documented allocation (IPCC 2022). Although the Adaptation Gap Report of the United Nations Environment Programme (UNEP) estimated annual adaptation costs in developing countries at $70 billion–$300 billion in 2018–2019 (UNEP 2021), only $40.8 billion was allocated, according to the CPI's Global Landscape of Climate Finance (2019a, 2020). Adaptation finance therefore covered less than half of adaptation needs and would not reach the 2030 target without a fundamental change, thus showing the necessity of scaling up adaptation finance.

Among the five subregions, East Asia was still the biggest recipient and provider of climate finance in 2018–2019. It received 80% of total finance tracked in this report, and placed the greater part in mitigation projects in the energy, transport, and building and infrastructure sectors, consistent with the PRC's plan to reach peak emissions by 2030 and achieve its carbon neutrality target by 2060. Next highest were climate finance flows to South Asia (9% of the regional total) and Southeast Asia (5%), mainly in support of clean energy, railway systems, and integrated urban public transportation. Central and West Asia, for its part, channeled its share (2%) into energy transformation, security, and resiliency. Meanwhile, the 0.3% share of the Pacific was directed in almost equal portions at mitigation and adaptation measures for land and marine conservation, and disaster risk management (DRM). All subregions in Asia and the Pacific except for the Pacific emphasized mitigation finance, mainly to transform energy systems and have significant impact on GHG emissions per dollar value.

Domestic finance, mainly from national DFIs, rose significantly in 2018–2019 and made up 87% of total flows allocated and spent within each country during the period. Domestic climate finance was concentrated in East Asia (80% of total flows), and most of this was spent in the PRC. The second-largest recipient was South Asia (9% of the total), with the majority of the finance going to India. Investment in local projects was apparently perceived to carry less risk because of market familiarity and preference. Although the PRC and India were undeniably bigger economies and had stronger local government support, making them better able to mobilize climate finance, local funding sources were easier to access than international sources, which required compliance with tailored and complex safeguard requirements. Given the current inadequacy of climate finance flows, more international finance could be tapped if local entities were to have greater capacity and readiness to access it.

Most climate finance was raised in the form of debt instruments, which amounted to $366.6 billion, or 70% of total finance. Market-rate debt dominated and was generally provided by national DFIs at the project level, highlighting the continued scarcity of concessional debt, even from development institutions. The remaining debt was issued through balance sheets, mainly by corporations, for renewable energy projects, while a minor amount of low-cost project-level debt was issued by public institutions to initiate early project development. The other financial instruments identified were: (i) equity placement (25%) by corporations, public entities, and households; (ii) grants (4%) for project planning and implementation and policy support; and (iii) finance for capacity building (1%).

The figure below summarizes the state of climate finance in the Asia and Pacific region in the 2018–2019 period—its sources and intermediaries, the financial instruments used, the types of activities financed, and the beneficiary sectors.

Total Climate Finance Flows to Asia and the Pacific, 2018–2019
($ billion)

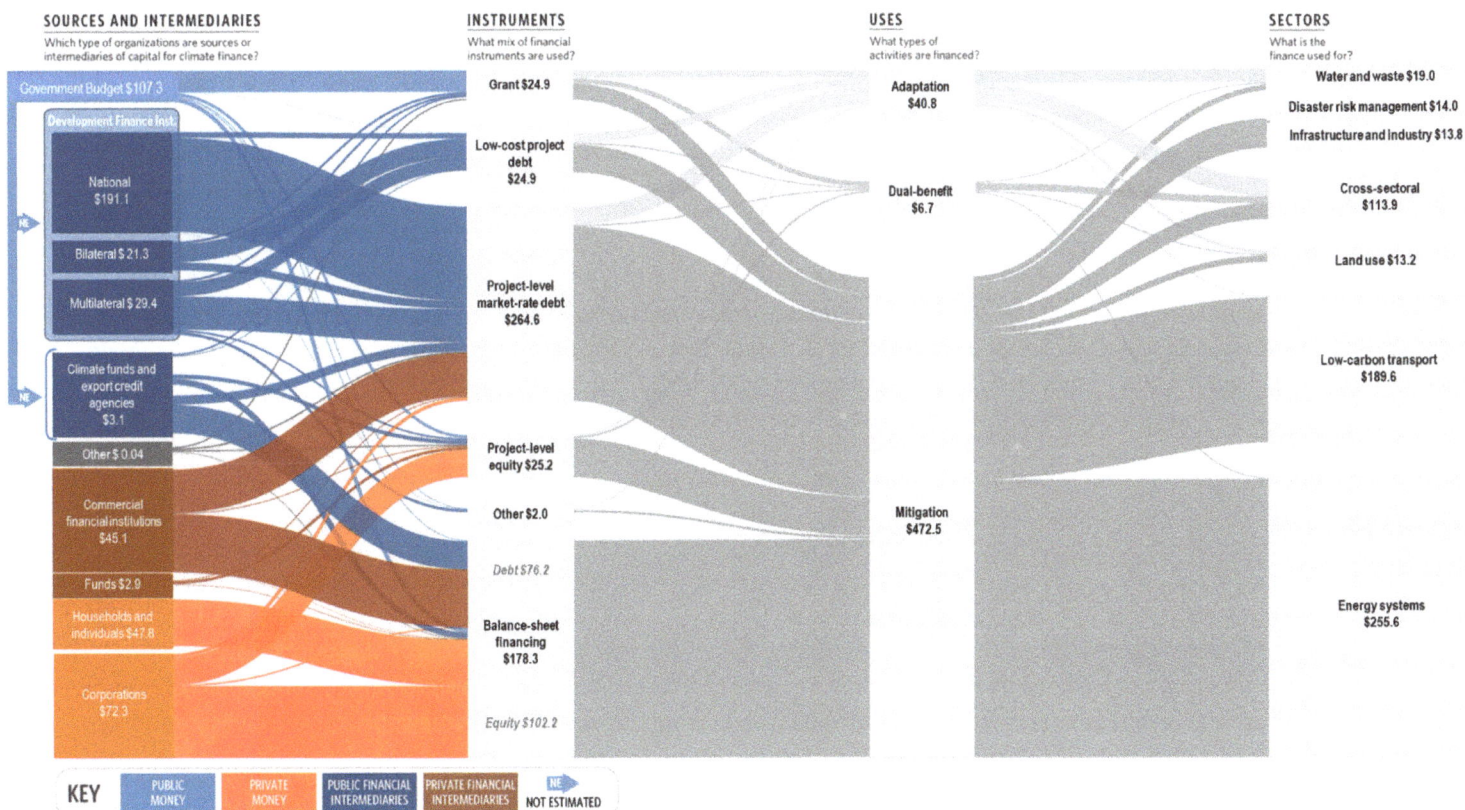

Source: Authors' compilation.

Subregional Climate Finance Landscapes

Central and West Asia. In 2018–2019, 2% ($12.4 billion) of climate finance flows to Asia and the Pacific went to this subregion. More than half of the projects, targeted mostly at energy system transformation, were funded from public sources ($7.8 billion). The total climate investment needed up to 2030 has been estimated at $186 billion, mainly for mitigation measures. Adaptation finance (20% of the estimated total investment) would be set aside for agriculture and for DRM projects, such as hydrometeorology and disaster risk reduction, to improve weather forecasting and flood warning systems.

Central and West Asia is the center of the world's fossil fuel production and reserves, making it more difficult for this subregion to shift to low-carbon growth. Governments should therefore find effective ways to mobilize climate finance for projects with the most impact on emission reduction and resilience to climate change. Detailed information about climate investment in the subregion, such as domestic public and private finance, has not been made fully available, despite an increase in the amount of its climate finance. For UNFCCC reporting, Central and West Asian countries report only the financing received from global climate funds. The whole range of climate-related projects is not fully considered.

East Asia. Eighty percent ($418.1 billion) of Asia and Pacific climate finance in the 2018–2019 period w as raised and spent mainly in the East Asia subregion and targeted at the energy and low-carbon transport sectors, reflecting the PRC's plan to reach peak emissions by 2030 and attain its carbon neutrality target by 2060. Climate finance came mostly from the domestic public sector—national DFIs, local governments, and state-owned enterprises (SOEs). As one of the world's biggest economies and carbon dioxide emitters, East Asia needs up to $14,012 billion in clima te investments to reach its NDC target by 2030.

Adaptation finance accounted for only 6% of the subregion's climate finance total in 2018–2019; the lar gest share of this allocation went to water and wastewater (55%) and cross-sectoral projects (44%). The 6% figure is most likely an underestimation, considering the potential adaptation benefits of ecological construction, water management, and other sustainability projects, as well as the difficulties in tracking adaptation finance among private entities.

South Asia. The subregion received 9% ($46.8 billion) of climate finance in Asia and the Pacific in 2018–2019. Climate-related projects funded from public sources accounted for more than half ($26.5 billion, or 56%) and were largely aimed at climate mitigation (83% of total climate-related projects). Total climate investment needed to meet the subregion's NDC target has been estimated at $2,727 billion. Local governments were progressing toward energy system transformation (mostly with the help of solar PV and onshore wind technologies); some long-term strategy scenarios showed the subregion, particularly India, far outpacing the rest of the world in renewable energy growth.

Several South Asian countries have made strides in developing climate finance tracking systems: three out of eight countries in the subregion have conducted the Climate Public Expenditure and Institutional Review. However, the lack of a standardized or internationally agreed definition and taxonomy for climate finance, methodological limitations, and low institutional capacity hinder extensive tracking. For instance, low-income countries do not have the institutional capacity and resources to conduct a comprehensive assessment of climate financing needs and flows. Without standardized and mandatory disclosure frameworks, private investments cannot be tracked or only limited tracking can be done.

Southeast Asia. The subregion had a 5% share of climate finance in Asia and the Pacific in 2018–2019 ($2 7.8 billion), most of it sourced through DFIs—national, multilateral, and bilateral. ADB, the biggest contributor, provided about one-third of tracked finance from multilateral sources.

The NDCs of countries in the subregion emphasize the urgency of shifting from fossil fuel–based energy to cleaner energy generation, to increase the share of renewable energy sources in the energy mix by 2030. This emphasis is also reflected in the CPI's Global Landscape (CPI 2019a), wher e mitigation finance accounts for 84% of climate finance. Despite being one of the most vulnerable subregions, however, Southeast Asia obtained adaptation finance amounting to only 12% of its climate finance total in 2018–2019, mainly to finance priority sectors such as land use change and forestry, natural resource management, and water and wastewater management, and to strengthen institutional capacity. Adaptation finance remains a challenging issue in the subregion because of its fragmented nature and the difficulty of getting precise and granular finance-related data. The result is uneven adaptation–mitigation funding, and limited capacity of countries to reverse the effects of climate change and to improve the resilience of vulnerable populations.

Pacific. Only 0.3% (or $1.4 billion) of climate finance in Asia and the Pacific in 2018–2019 flowed to this subregion, and was accessible either directly through bilateral donors and multilateral development banks or through multilateral climate funds. The geographic concentration of the population in the coastal áreas increases the subregion's exposure to climate adaptation impact. To meet its 2030 NDC target, the Pacific needs climate investment of $5.2 billion, including $1 billion for building coastal protection infrastructure.

Strong international support combining mitigation, adaptation, and dual-benefit finance, in nearly equal portions, has been received from multilateral DFIs (e.g., the Green Climate Fund, the Global Environment Facility), international climate and public funds, and foreign governments. Mitigation finance is generally directed at the renewable energy and low-carbon transport sectors; adaptation finance, at biodiversity, land, and marine conservation, DRM, and policy support. The CPI's Global Landscape (CPI 2019a) notes the minimal amount of tracked finance in the Pacific, sourced from national budgets (less than 1% of climate finance in the subregion). This indicates the low availability of climate finance and inadequate disclosure of climate data by governments, highlighting the importance of strengthening national policies for climate finance tracking and tagging.

Challenges and Opportunities in Mobilizing Climate Finance in Asia and the Pacific

Despite an increase in 2018–2019, the current level of climate finance in Asia and the Pacific is not enough to keep global warming below 1.5°C and support countries in increasing their resilience in the face of intensifying climate impact. Deep-dive analyses of some region- and country-specific contexts suggest key challenges contributing to suboptimal mobilization of climate finance in Asia and the Pacific:

- Insufficient effort is being made to address climate adaptation.
- All the five subregions—Central and West Asia, East Asia, South Asia, Southeast Asia, and the Pacific—still rely mainly on fossil fuels to drive their economies, making the low-carbon transition a key challenge.
- Climate finance flows, classified according to use and sector, region, and source, are insufficient and disproportionate,a despite a 31% incr ease in finance in 2018–2019.
- Limited access to long-term finance, especially for small-scale climate projects, constrains the capacity to attract sufficient investment to the sector, region, or country where it is needed most.
- There are gaps in institutional capacity and arrangements for access to climate finance.
- Capacity gaps in tracking and reporting of climate finance, and lack of transparency and disclosure, may result in an incomplete assessment of the effectiveness and impact of climate finance.

Aside from these key challenges, the fallout from the COVID-19 pandemic laid bare the structural vulnerabilities affecting climate finance flows in 2020, especially in developing countries. Globally, total climate finance has steadily increased over the last decade, reaching $632 billion in 2019–2020, but flows have slowed in the last few years, particularly in 2020, when COVID-19 broke out (CPI 2021). The CPI's Global Landscape of Climate Finance indicates an annual increase in climate finance flows of only 10% between 2017–2018 and 2019–2020, much lower than the 24% growth achieved in previous periods.

Understanding the climate finance landscape of Asia and the Pacific helps governments and development partners to identify barriers, and address these to support the transition toward low-carbon and climate-resilient development. To accelerate and scale up climate finance across the region, some opportunities could be capitalized on:

- Ensuring that climate finance is available, sufficient, and accessible, and is targeted at underserved regions, countries, and sectors with the most impact on achieving NDC targets, by
  - » streamlining the coordination of the public and private sectors in carrying out their climate finance roles and responsibilities;
  - » redirecting the regulatory framework, e.g., by mainstreaming climate targets into national planning and policy, and defining oversight mechanisms among government agencies; and
  - » leveraging the fiscal capacity of governments, through subsidies, tax incentives, public–private partnerships, and other means, to attract private investors by mitigating the financial risks and influencing financial regulation to crowd in private sector finance for climate action (e.g., regulation classifying climate-related activities, and regulation setting a minimum proportion of bank lending for climate projects).
- Improving understanding of climate finance effectiveness and impact, to achieve the highest value for every dollar flow.
- Overcoming barriers to long-term financing.
- Enhancing transparency and capacity for climate finance tracking and reporting.
- Improving the capacity of governments to plan and mobilize resources on the basis of climate finance data,
- e.g., by identifying financing gaps, for better alignment with their climate policy objectives.

1   Background

The Asia and Pacific region is vulnerable to the impact of the climate crisis and plays a key role in keeping global warming within 1.5°C. The region is considered significantly more vulnerable to the impact of climate change than other regions worldwide. The severe impact of a breach of the 1.5°C threshold on regions and people with considerable development constraints has been pointed out by the Intergovernmental Panel on Climate Change (IPCC 2022). Parts of Asia and the Pacific are already experiencing an increase in extreme-weather disasters that are compounding the developmental challenges faced by much of the region, including food insecurity, child malnutrition, and low access to decent health care and sanitation. The region must be better prepared for this impact and more resilient to climate change.

Meanwhile, in 2019, the region's share to global emissions has increased by over 60% above 2010 lev els or a record high of 36.7 $GtCO_2e$ which comprises over 60% of total global emissions in 2019 (UNESCAP et al 2021). Emissions decreased to 35 $GtCO_2e$ in 2020, amid the economic slowdown due to the COVID-19 pandemic, but is expected to rise to 50 $GTCO_2e$ by 2060 (UNESCAP et al 2021). A popula tion increase is also projected for Asia and the Pacific by 2030, to at least 4.3 billion, or 60% of the world total (ADB 2019).

Under current conditions, Asian countries are predominantly categorized as "highly insufficient" to meet the global targets set under the Paris Agreement (Climate Action Tracker 2021). They must urgently step up their climate action, given the need to reduce their significant share of emissions and slow down the rate of increase.

Meeting the global target of keeping warming within 1.5°C and aligning with the goal set in the Paris Agreement will require vast investment and more strategic investment planning. Up to $16,999.3 billion[1] will have to be invested between now and 2030 to meet the region's Nationally Determined Contribution (NDC) targets; for the climate-proofing of infrastructure alone, the required investments will amount to 3.3% of gross domestic product (GDP) (Fouad et al. 2021). Current global investment levels must therefore increase by at least 454%, or by $4.1 trillion (CPI 2020). Moreover, given that a number of developing countries of the Asia Development Bank (ADB) have committed themselves to net-zero goal, the total financing needed to meet Paris Agreement targets will be even higher than current estimates suggest. The developing countries must manage and allocate their resources efficiently to finance more ambitious and long-term climate action.

In November 2021, the United Nations Framework Convention on Climate Change (UNFCCC) Conference of the Parties (COP26) reached consensus on key measures to strengthen action on climate change. One of these measures was fulfilling the pledge made by developed countries to provide $100 billion per year in climate finance to developing countries. So far, this pledge has not been met.

---

[1]   This estimate is based on investment needs for climate change mitigation or adaptation, or both, in accordance with the commitments made by 38 developing countries in their NDCs (see Appendix Table A5).

Meanwhile, developing countries were being asked to strengthen their ambitions and translate their NDCs into climate investment plans. Though Asia and the Pacific is the largest recipient and spender of climate finance, uneven finance flows across regions and sectors within Asia result in unequal capacity to mitigate emissions and respond to climate impact (Barnard et al. 2015). This has become a key challenge, as the region will require synergy and concerted effort to access funds equitably and optimize climate finance flows. Joint efforts must be streamlined and coordinated to achieve scale in climate finance for targeted sectors and countries.

The landscape of climate finance flowing to and within Asia and the Pacific must be better understood and the extent to which financing decisions promote the achievement of the region's collective climate ambitions must be assessed. This report aims to provide a more detailed picture of the climate finance landscape of Asia and the Pacific by evaluating the sources of climate finance and its intended destination sectors and activities, disaggregated for each subregion. Capacity gaps in financial tracking and specific challenges in accessing and mobilizing finance in ADB's developing countries in Asia and the Pacific are also brought out here.

For governments, the assessment of finance flows is a useful tool for comparing performance against climate commitments, to improve decision-making and achieve better alignment of resource allocation and use with climate policy objectives. To align their climate financing with the Paris Agreement, governments must know which financial flows are consistent with the Agreement's goals, and which ones are not (CPI 2019a). The assessment can also promote knowledge exchange and sharing of lessons from successful or well-mobilized climate financing, including experience with innovative mechanisms. In addition, it can add value to information flowing toward the global stocktake that will take place every 5 years, starting in 2023, helping to strengthen support for managing climate loss and damage in affected countries.[2]

---

[2]   The global stocktake of the Paris Agreement (GST) is a process of taking stock of the implementation of the agreement and assessing the world's collective progress toward achieving the purposes of the agreement and its long-term goals (Article 14).

2 Methods and Approaches

The climate finance landscape in Asia and the Pacific was assessed in four main steps (Figure 1).

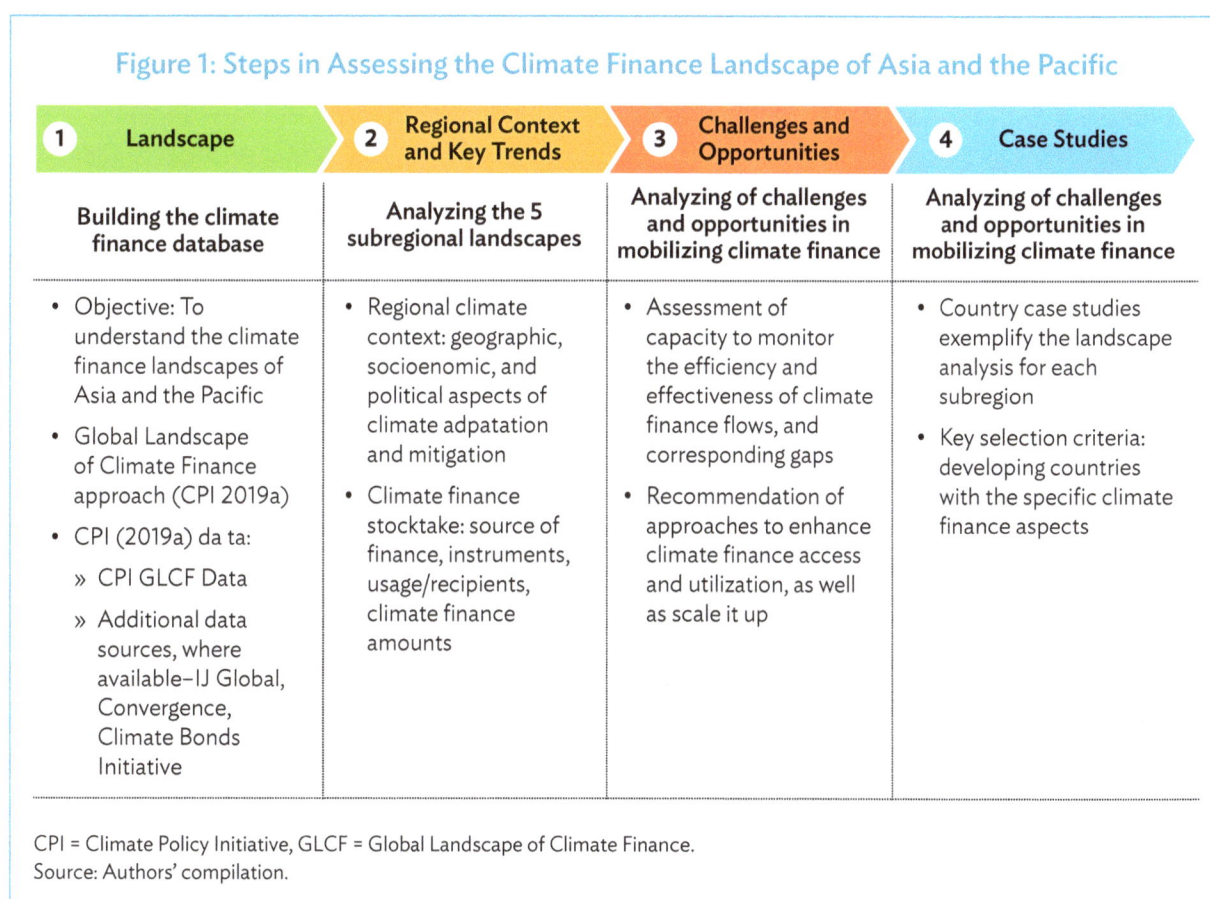

Figure 1: Steps in Assessing the Climate Finance Landscape of Asia and the Pacific

1 Landscape	2 Regional Context and Key Trends	3 Challenges and Opportunities	4 Case Studies
Building the climate finance database	**Analyzing the 5 subregional landscapes**	**Analyzing of challenges and opportunities in mobilizing climate finance**	**Analyzing of challenges and opportunities in mobilizing climate finance**

• Objective: To understand the climate finance landscapes of Asia and the Pacific
• Global Landscape of Climate Finance approach (CPI 2019a)
• CPI (2019a) da ta:
  » CPI GLCF Data
  » Additional data sources, where available–IJ Global, Convergence, Climate Bonds Initiative
	• Regional climate context: geographic, socioenomic, and political aspects of climate adpatation and mitigation
	• Climate finance stocktake: source of finance, instruments, usage/recipients, climate finance amounts
		• Assessment of capacity to monitor the efficiency and effectiveness of climate finance flows, and corresponding gaps
		• Recommendation of approaches to enhance climate finance access and utilization, as well as scale it up
			• Country case studies exemplify the landscape analysis for each subregion
			• Key selection criteria: developing countries with the specific climate finance aspects

CPI = Climate Policy Initiative, GLCF = Global Landscape of Climate Finance.
Source: Authors' compilation.

The first step was building a database on climate finance in Asia and the Pacific, from the global to the domestic level, using the *Climate Policy Initiative's Global Landscape of Climate Finance* (CPI 2019a, 2020, 2021) and data from national tracking initiatives, such as India's Landscape of Green Finance, Indonesia's Landscape of Private Climate Finance, and the Landscape of Climate Finance of the People's Republic of China (PRC). On the basis of the landscape data, key financial trends in primary flows directed toward low-carbon and climate-resilient development interventions with direct or indirect greenhouse gas mitigation or adaptation benefits were assessed for this report.

The CPI's Global Landscape (CPI 2019a) brings together data from a wide range of primary and secondary sources, capturing information on primary financing support for greenhouse gas emission reduction and climate resilience activities. It follows financial flows throughout their life cycle, from their original sourcing to their deployment, through financial intermediaries, in the form of financial instruments to the recipients of finance, and the ultimate use of the funds.[1]

The second step was conducting deep-dive research into the five Asia and Pacific subregions—Central and West Asia, East Asia, South Asia, Southeast Asia, and the Pacific. This step involved (i) describing the subregional climate context, such as the geographic, socioeconomic, and political aspects of climate adaptation and mitigation; and (ii) taking stock of climate finance, its sources (e.g., government, private), instruments (e.g., loans, grants), use and sector allocation (e.g., adaptation/mitigation, sectors/subsectors), and disaggregated and aggregated climate finance amounts, where data were available.

The third step was identifying the challenges and opportunities in monitoring the efficiency and effectiveness of climate finance flows in Asia and the Pacific, and the corresponding gaps. Identifying potential entry points for more effective tracking of climate finance flows led to recommended approaches to enhancing climate finance access and use by the countries in the region. Specific analyses of challenges, opportunities, and gaps, covering the five subregions, are presented in this report.

The fourth and last step was developing case studies for each subregion in Asia and the Pacific. The case studies demonstrated best practices in accessing, mobilizing, and scaling up climate finance, and were selected on the basis of available data on countries or subregions that had manifested or made significant progress in their climate finance programs.

The financial landscape analysis accounted for financial flows from public and private sources and captured the aggregate analysis of the five subregions. The assessment of financial flows from public finance stakeholders covered multilateral, bilateral, and national development finance institutions (DFIs); government spending; and multilateral and national climate funds. Private finance stakeholders consisted of corporate actors, households, commercial financial institutions (e.g., commercial and investment banks), and institutional investors (insurance companies, asset management firms, pension funds, foundations, and endowments).

The financial tracking for 2018–2019 made use of various databases to capture the landscape of finance flows in Asia and the Pacific, including the main financing sources (e.g., public or private; investors, banks, or donors), the financial instruments used (e.g., grants, debt instruments, corporate financing, project financing), and the use of the proceeds (e.g., mitigation/adaptation/cross-sectoral, projects). The tracking (i) recorded primary investments in productive assets and projects that contributed directly to adaptation or mitigation, or both; (ii) captured commitments, not disbursements; and (iii) excluded secondary market transactions, policy-induced revenue support mechanisms, or other public subsidies with the primary function of paying back investment cost, or investing in manufacturing, sales, research and development, and fossil fuel–based lower-carbon and energy-efficient generation. Figure 2 illustrates the climate finance flow, and Table 1 lists the 38 countries included in this assessment, based on ADB's subregional groupings of its 38 developing countries.

---

[1]   The CPI's *Global Landscape of Climate Finance 2021*, published in December 2021, contains 2019–2020 data. However, 2018–2019 data are mainly used in this report because of primary-data limitations in the 2021 CPI publication: (i) the 2019–2020 data are aggregated data, lacking in granularity; and (ii) the nonavailability of country-level data could affect the depth of this report's regional assessment.

Figure 2: Snapshot of Climate Finance Flows in Asia and the Pacific, 2018–2019

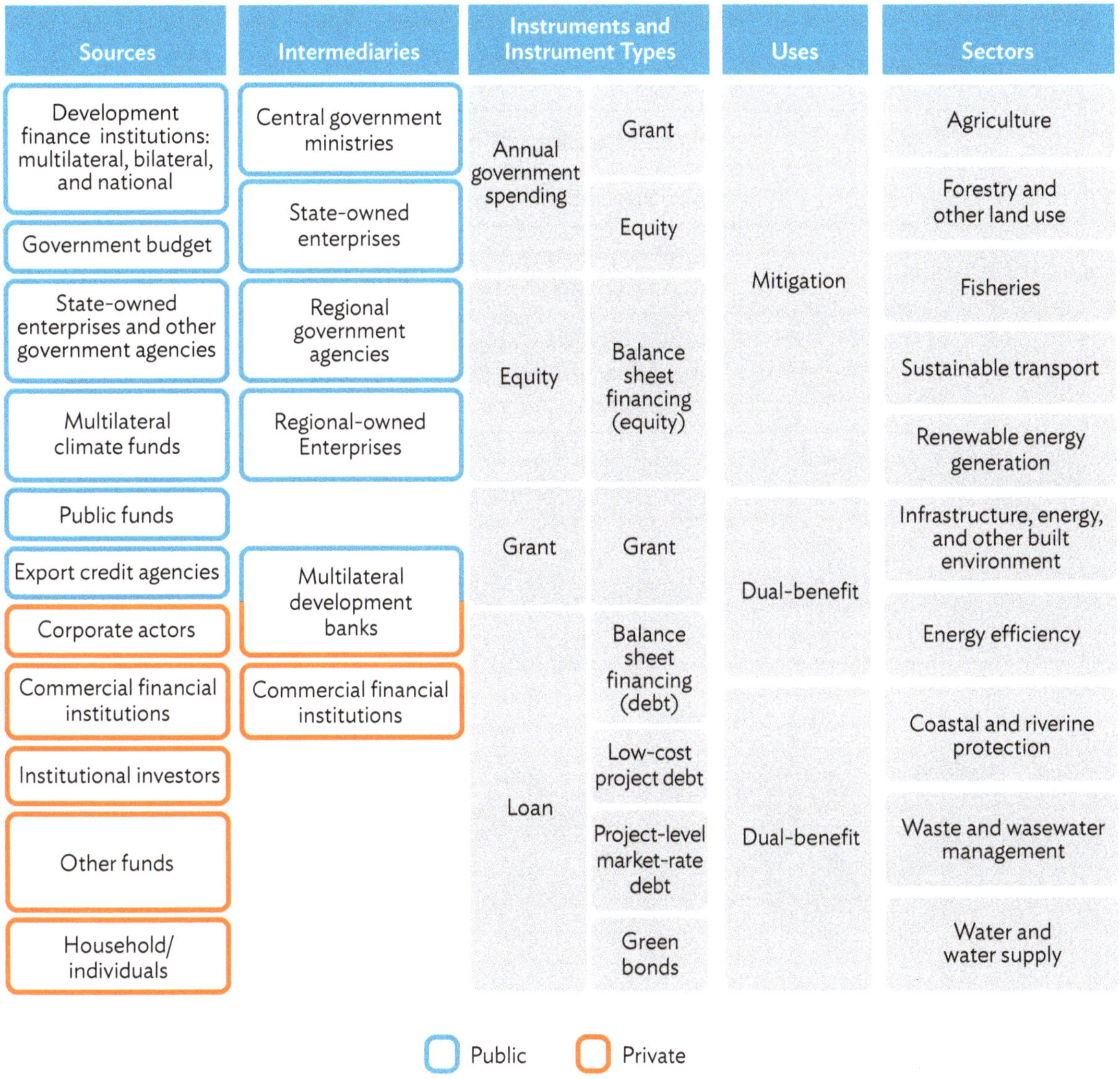

Sources	Intermediaries	Instruments and Instrument Types		Uses	Sectors
Development finance institutions: multilateral, bilateral, and national	Central government ministries	Annual government spending	Grant	Mitigation	Agriculture
Government budget	State-owned enterprises		Equity		Forestry and other land use
State-owned enterprises and other government agencies	Regional government agencies	Equity	Balance sheet financing (equity)		Fisheries
Multilateral climate funds	Regional-owned Enterprises				Sustainable transport
					Renewable energy generation
Public funds		Grant	Grant		Infrastructure, energy, and other built environment
Export credit agencies	Multilateral development banks			Dual-benefit	
Corporate actors			Balance sheet financing (debt)		Energy efficiency
Commercial financial institutions	Commercial financial institutions		Low-cost project debt		Coastal and riverine protection
Institutional investors		Loan	Project-level market-rate debt	Dual-benefit	Waste and wasewater management
Other funds			Green bonds		Water and water supply
Household/ individuals					

◻ Public   ◻ Private

Source: Authors' compilation.

Table 1: Subregional Groupings of ADB Developing Countries in Asia and the Pacific

Subregion	ADB Developing Countries
Central and West Asia	Armenia, Azerbaijan, Georgia, Kazakhstan, Kyrgyz Republic, Pakistan, Tajikistan, Turkmenistan, and Uzbekistan
East Asia	People's Republic of China and Mongolia
South Asia	Bangladesh, Bhutan, India, Maldives, Nepal, and Sri Lanka
Southeast Asia	Cambodia, Indonesia, Lao People's Democratic Republic, Philippines, Thailand, Timor-Leste, and Viet Nam
Pacific	Cook Islands, Federated States of Micronesia, Fiji, Kiribati, Marshall Islands, Nauru, Niue, Palau, Papua New Guinea, Samoa, Solomon Islands, Tonga, Tuvalu, and Vanuatu

ADB = Asian Development Bank.
Source: ADB (2022).

Box 1: Data Limitations and Gaps in Climate Finance Tracking for 38 Developing Countries in 2018–2019

The quality of tracked data affects the ability to capture more granular information from various databases. Data sets for the landscape assessment are mostly sourced from direct surveys of the International Development Finance Club (IDFC) and Bloomberg New Energy Finance (BNEF). The data include primary-investment into productive assets at the project level with direct contribution to climate adaptation or mitigation, or both, and excludes (i) secondary market flows (transactions where money changes hands, but with no physical impact) and research and development spending assumed to be recovered through the sale of the resulting products; and (ii) finance provided through some financial instruments such as guarantees, insurance, government revenue support schemes, and fiscal incentives. This approach seeks to arrive at a non-double-counted estimate of financial flows, cross-referenced to literature reviews. Addressing these remaining gaps as highlighted in the Global Landscape (CPI 2019a) could improve the granularity of data:

- **Domestic public climate finance from governments.** While several countries are undertaking climate finance tracking activities, data limitations prevent a full accounting of public budgets dedicated to domestic climate action, particularly domestic public procurement or infrastructure investment and the government's share in the investments of state-owned enterprises.

- **Private climate finance.** Publicly available data on private climate finance, and particularly on adaptation finance, are limited, for confidentiality reasons. Keyword searches and news articles are therefore used to capture the information.

- **Adaptation finance.** There are constraints on defining adaptation-relevant activities, and universally accepted impact metrics for adaptation finance are lacking (UNFCCC 2018; CPI 2019a). Particularly within mobilized private finance data sets, the relevant adaptation investments are often components within larger projects, requiring disaggregated information that is unlikely to be reported voluntarily by private financiers. Moreover, for adaptation finance to be effective, the activities must be consistent with climate-resilient pathways and not just represent an arbitrary improvement over business as usual. Therefore, to assess consistency, reporting on progress against benchmarks or standards is required. Currently, benchmarks are still insufficient for clear indicator and impact metrics for adaptation. The main reasons are (i) difficulty in defining and tagging the expected outcomes of an adaptation finance flow because of the context dependence of most adaptation finance (specific regional or local vulnerabilities determine the adaptation and resilience outcomes of an investment) (AfDB et al. 2018a); and (ii) uncertainty of causality links, resulting in technical challenges in developing links between adaptation and resilience outcomes and development impact. Data currently disclosed fall short of providing such degree of detail.

Because of these data limitations and gaps, the resulting numbers in this report present a conservative estimate of climate finance in Asia and the Pacific.

Source: Global Landscape (CPI 2019a).

3 Climate Finance Landscape of Asia and the Pacific

Climate finance in Asia and the Pacific in 2018–2019 totaled $519.9 billion—$225.6 billion in 2018 and $294.3 billion (30% more) in 2019 (Figure 3). The increase occurred mostly in finance for renewable energy generation (52% of the total) and low-carbon transportation (34%) (see breakdown by sector, Figure 4). The greater part of public finance during the period went to East Asia (81% of the total), mainly to the PRC (see breakdown by region, Figure 3).

Figure 3: Climate Finance in Asia and the Pacific, by Subregion, 2018–2019
($ billion)

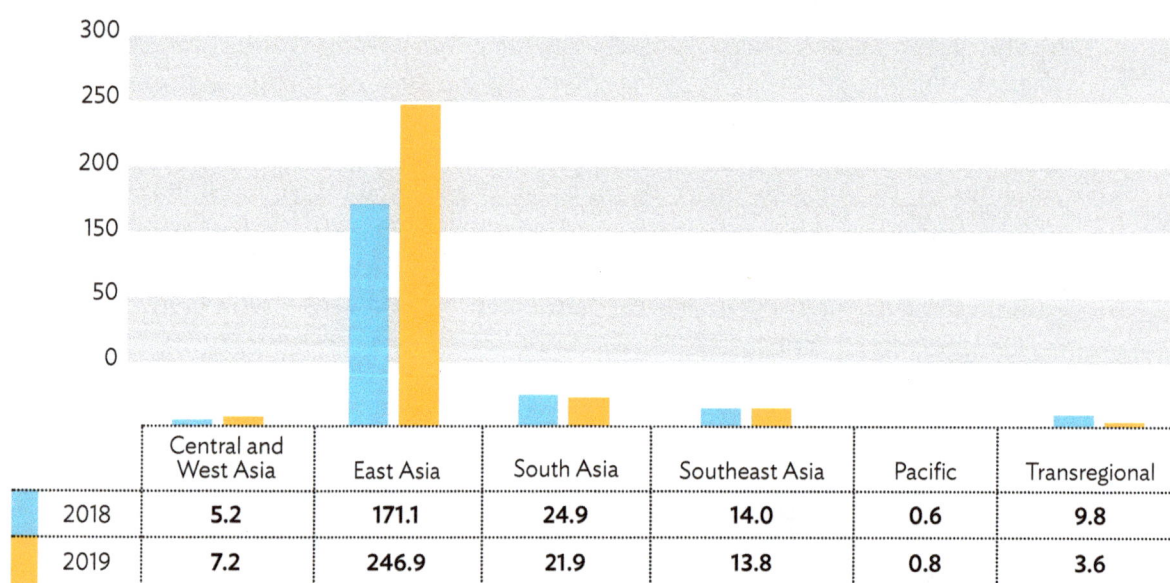

	Central and West Asia	East Asia	South Asia	Southeast Asia	Pacific	Transregional
2018	5.2	171.1	24.9	14.0	0.6	9.8
2019	7.2	246.9	21.9	13.8	0.8	3.6

Note: Transregional finance flows are flows associated with more than one of the five subregions in Asia and the Pacific. All transregional finance in 2018–2019 came from the public sector, and was intended mainly for mitigation activities in the energy and transport sectors, as well as across sectors (e.g., building and infrastructure, industry, water and wastewater, and agriculture, forestry, and land use).

Source: Authors' compilation.

Figure 4: Climate Finance in Asia and the Pacific, by Subregion and Sector, 2018–2019
($ billion)

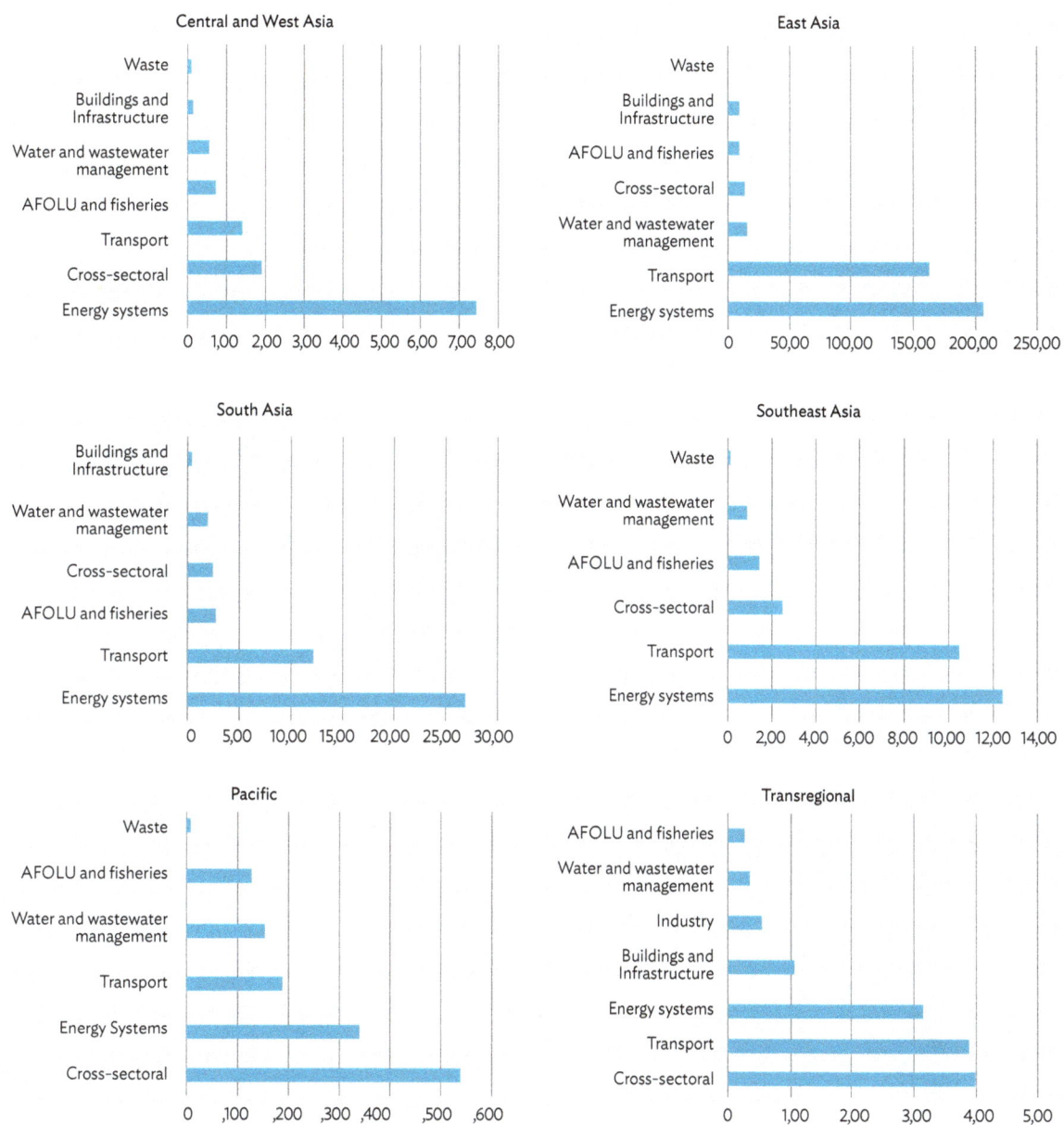

AFOLU = agriculture, forestry, and land use.
Source: Authors' compilation.

3.1   Sources and Intermediaries

Various databases were used in climate finance tracking to capture the finance flow, including the sources of the financing, e.g., public (DFIs, government budgets and agencies) or private (corporations, institutional investors, banks).

3.1.1 Public Finance

Public finance amounting to $351.8 billion (68% of the total flow) was the main source of climate finance in Asia and the Pacific in 2018–2019. Mitigation finance made up 91%; adaptation finance, 8%; and dual-benefit finance, 1%. DFIs (multilateral, bilateral, and national), government spending, and multilateral and national and climate funds were the identified public finance stakeholders. Climate finance from public sources increased by 48% in 2018–2019, from $142.0 billion to $209.8 billion. The public sources and intermediaries of climate finance during the period are presented in Figure 5.

Figure 5: Public Sources and Intermediaries of Climate Finance in Asia and the Pacific, 2018–2019
($ billion)

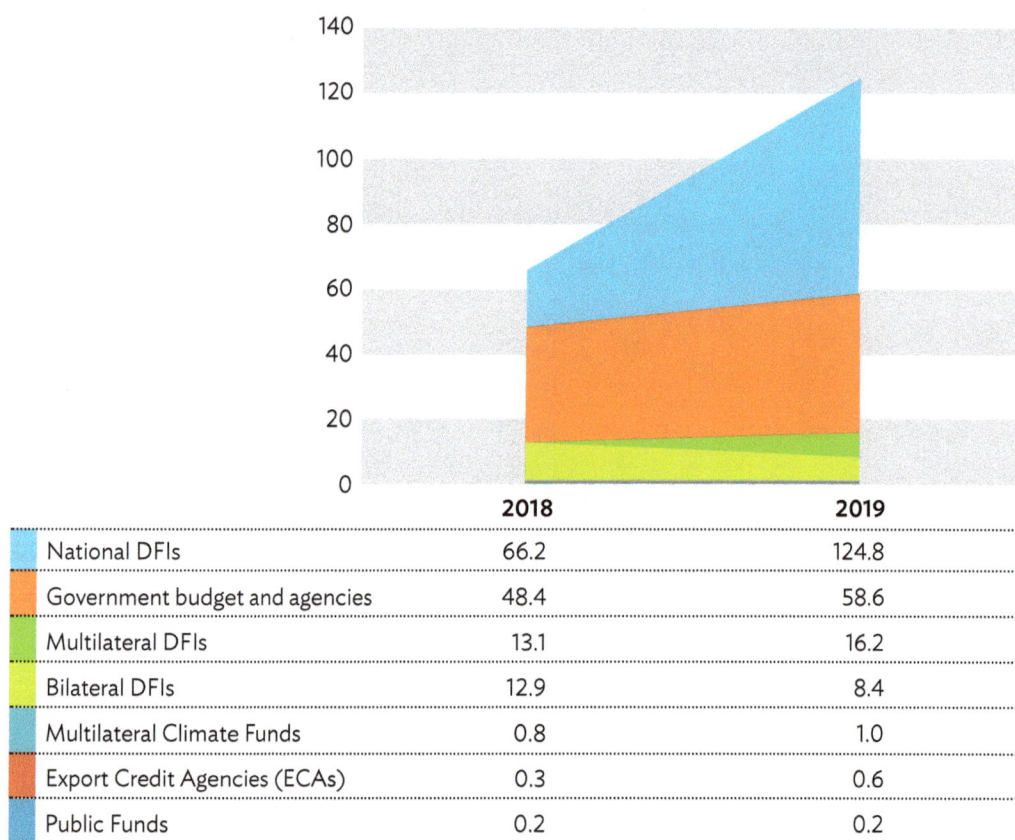

	2018	2019
National DFIs	66.2	124.8
Government budget and agencies	48.4	58.6
Multilateral DFIs	13.1	16.2
Bilateral DFIs	12.9	8.4
Multilateral Climate Funds	0.8	1.0
Export Credit Agencies (ECAs)	0.3	0.6
Public Funds	0.2	0.2

Source: Authors' compilation.

DFIs were the key contributors, accounting for $241.7 billion (68% of the public finance total) in 2018–2019. Among these institutions, national DFIs contributed the most—their commitments rose from $66.2 billion in 2018 to $124.8 billion (88% higher) in 2019—followed by multilateral DFIs, which increased their commitments by 20%, from $13.1 billion to $16.2 billion. The spike was driven by clean energy financing (power and heat transmission and distribution). Bilateral DFIs, on the other hand, reduced their financing by $4.5 billion (−35%) in 2019 with the shift in financing trend from the agriculture, forestry, and land use (AFOLU) and fisheries sectors to the energy sector, particularly in South Asia and Southeast Asia.

DFI finance flows to the energy sector accord with the rising demand for energy access and security in Asia and the Pacific. Although the region's improved electrification rate of 95.6% in 2018 indicates that the energy market is close to saturation, there is a push to accelerate the transition to cleaner energy systems. The region has developed considerable renewable energy capacity across a variety of technologies, mainly in solar and wind, as well as hydropower, geothermal, and bio-based energy. Particularly in the PRC, where most finance comes from national DFIs, renewable energy capacity has reached 758.6 GW, with 35% of the world's solar capacity and 34% of its wind capacity in 2019 (IRENA 2020).

Government budget and agency commitments continued to increase, from $48.4 billion in 2018 to $58.6 billion in 2019, accounting for 30% of public finance flows. The increase was attributable to government spending for transport and energy systems, driven by the country's pledge, made through the UNFCCC process and national policy commitments, to meet national climate targets for both emission reduction and energy sector decarbonization.

Multilateral climate funds and public funds provided a steady amount of finance during the period, contributing $898 million and $236 million per year, respectively, on average, while finance flows from export credit agencies increased from $314 million in 2018 to $555 million in 2019. The Green Climate Fund (GCF) confirmed that the largest share of its cumulative fund disbursements, amounting to $440 million in 2019 and $536 million in 2020 (36% of total GCF cumulative disbursements from 2016), went to Asia and the Pacific, for mitigation and adaptation finance. Energy access and power generation took up the largest portion of GCF mitigation-related funding, followed by buildings, cities, industries and appliances, and low-carbon transportation, reflecting the continuing trend of a dominant proportion of energy-related projects and programs.

In adaptation funding, the GCF emphasized health, food, and water security, followed by more resilient livelihoods for vulnerable people and communities, as well as infrastructure and the built environment and ecosystems better able to withstand the effects of climate change (GCF 2020, 2021). Of the public finance total, 12% was placed in adaptation finance, mainly for water security and sanitation, disaster risk management (DRM), as well as strengthening of the enabling environment, through policy support and other means. In 2020, the GCF financed regional adaptation projects with $47 million in grant support for five of the Pacific countries, to enhance climate information and knowledge services (Climate Funds Update 2021). The Least Development Countries Fund also approved $82 million in funding in 2020 for water and waste projects in the Pacific, the Lao People's Democratic Republic (Lao PDR), and Viet Nam (CFU 2021; GEF 2020). Table 2 lists various multilateral and public funds supporting Asia and the Pacific.

Table 2: Multilateral Funds Supporting Asia and the Pacific

• Green Climate Fund (GCF) • Least Developed Countries Fund (LDCF) • Pilot Program for Climate Resilience (PPCR) • Global Environment Facility (GEF) • Adaptation Fund • Global Climate Change Alliance (GCCA) • Nationally Appropriate Mitigation Actions (NAMA) Facility • Abu Dhabi Fund for Development (ADFD)	• Climate Change Fund (CCF) • Scaling Up Renewable Energy Program in Low Income Countries (SREP) • Forest Carbon Partnership Facility (FCPF) • Clean Technology Fund (CTF) • Special Climate Change Fund (SCCF) • United Nations Programme on Reducing Emissions from Deforestation and Forest Degradation (UN-REDD Programme) • Adaptation for Smallholder Agriculture Programme (ASAP) • Canadian Climate Fund for the Private Sector in Asia II (CFPS II)

Source: Adapted from IMF (2021).

3.1.2 Private Finance

Private finance of $168.1 billion in 2018–2019 represented 32% of total tracked finance during the period, almost all of it (99%) going to mitigation. The private finance stakeholders identified in the Global Landscape (CPI 2019a) ar e corporate entities, households, commercial financial institutions (e.g., commercial and investment banks), and institutional investors (insurance companies, asset management firms, pension funds, foundations, and endowments). The Global Landscape tracks direct primary investment by each stakeholder in climate-related infrastructure. Figure 6 provides summary information on the private sources and intermediaries of climate finance in 2018–2019.

Figure 6: Private Sources and Intermediaries of Climate Finance in Asia and the Pacific, 2018–2019
($ billion)

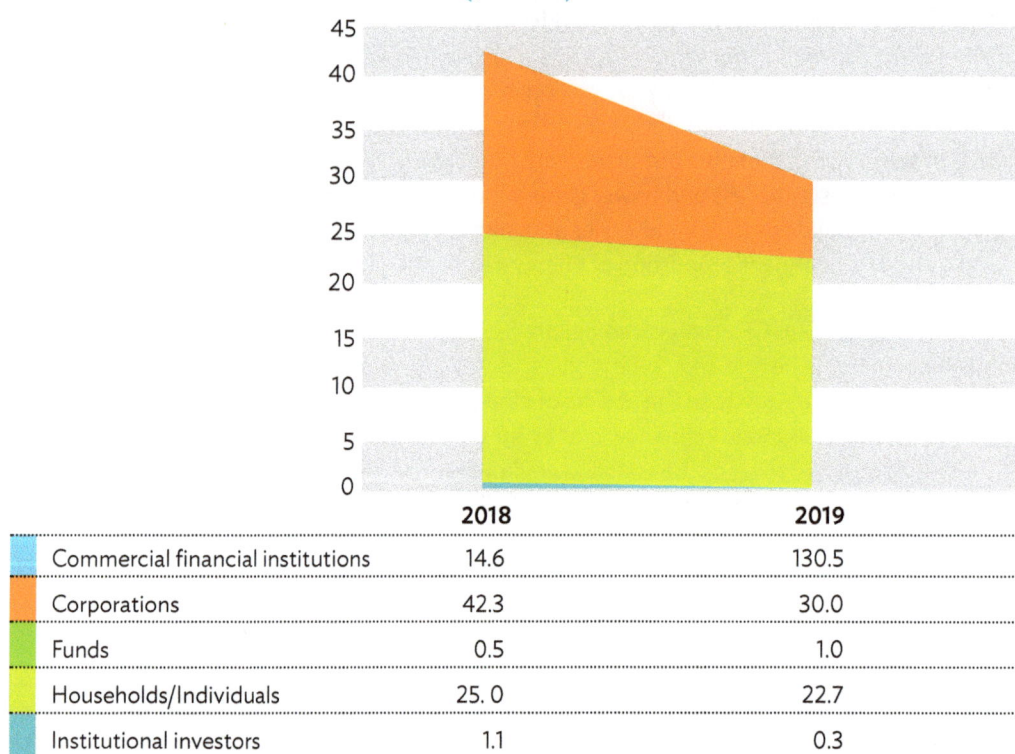

	2018	2019
Commercial financial institutions	14.6	130.5
Corporations	42.3	30.0
Funds	0.5	1.0
Households/Individuals	25. 0	22.7
Institutional investors	1.1	0.3

Source: Authors' compilation.

Corporations contributed a total of $72.3 billion, or 43% of total private finance, in 2018–2019. But the share of corporate contributions in total private finance decreased from 51% in 2018 to 35% in 2019 because of an increase in funding from other sources: (i) climate financing provided by commercial financial institutions, and (ii) spending by households on climate-related activities.

Households' climate-related spending of $47.8 billion in 2018–2019 made up 28% of total private finance during the period. This spending was attributable to the significant growth in the purchase of photovoltaic systems (PVs) for residential use (small-scale solar panels and solar water heaters) and electric vehicles.[2] For instance, Pakistan and Indonesia have adopted net-metering regulations to encourage the use of rooftop solar installations (IRENA

---

[2]   Only pure electric vehicles (battery electric vehicles) were purchased.

2019a, MEMR 2021, Wahid n.d.). The retail purchase of electric vehicles during the period was dominated by the PRC, where the electric-vehicle market is the world's largest.

Commercial financial institutions contributed $45.1 billion (27% of total private finance) in 2018–2019. The 2019 commitment ($30.5 billion) was more than double the amount they put in the year before ($14.6 billion). Most of this finance went to clean transport and renewable energy projects. This market trend affected the range of green banking instruments available, as banking products became more diverse and included specialized green products (e.g., solar PV loans, interest subsidy for agricultural projects), green bonds, and international green credit lines, such as ADB's green building program and the China Utility-Based Energy Efficiency Finance Program of the International Finance Corporation (IFC). Private funds (e.g., private equity, venture capital, infrastructure funds) and institutional investors provided a total of $1.5 billion and $1.3 billion, respectively, for project-level finance in 2018–2019.

Among the sectors, energy attracted the most private finance, with an increase in building and infrastructure financing from $65 million in 2018 to $10.9 billion in 2019. The increase was dominated by the growth of the heating, ventilation, and air conditioning industry, which accounted for 99% of total private finance in building and infrastructure development.

Only 0.1% of private finance went to adaptation finance, indicating that adaptation projects were perceived as lacking in well-developed markets and scalable business, and were therefore less financially attractive to private investors (IPCC 2022). Particularly within mobilized private finance, the relevant adaptation investments were often components within larger projects, some with dual (mitigation and adaptation) benefits. Disaggregating the adaptation component requires additional information, which private financiers were unlikely to report voluntarily, thus limiting the capture of data specific to adaptation.

3.2 Sectors

The Global Landscape (CPI 2019a) captures two primary climate finance flows—mitigation and adaptation. Mitigation finance is aimed at reducing greenhouse gas (GHG) emissions, to slow down global warming and stabilize the climate in the long term. Adaptation finance is focused on improving resiliency and reducing the impact of climate-related risk and damage. Some finance is targeted at projects and initiatives with both mitigation and adaptation outcomes (dual-benefit finance). Figure 7 shows the respective shares of mitigation, adaptation, and dual-benefit finance in Asia and the Pacific in 2018–2019.

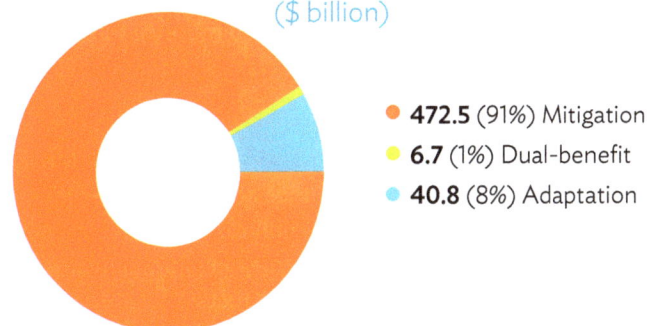

Figure 7: Mitigation, Adaptation, and Dual-Benefit Finance in Asia and the Pacific, 2018–2019
($ billion)

- **472.5** (91%) Mitigation
- **6.7** (1%) Dual-benefit
- **40.8** (8%) Adaptation

Source: Authors' compilation.

3.2.1 Mitigation Finance

Mitigation finance ($472.5 billion, or 91% of the total) dominated finance flows in 2018–2019, increasing by 32% from $203.9 billion in 2018 to $268.5 billion in 2019. Of the total amount set aside for climate mitigation, 64% ($304.7 billion) came from public sources, and 36% ($167.8 billion), from private sources. Figure 8 gives the sector breakdown of mitigation finance during the period.

Figure 8: Total Mitigation Finance in Asia and the Pacific, 2018–2019
($ billion)

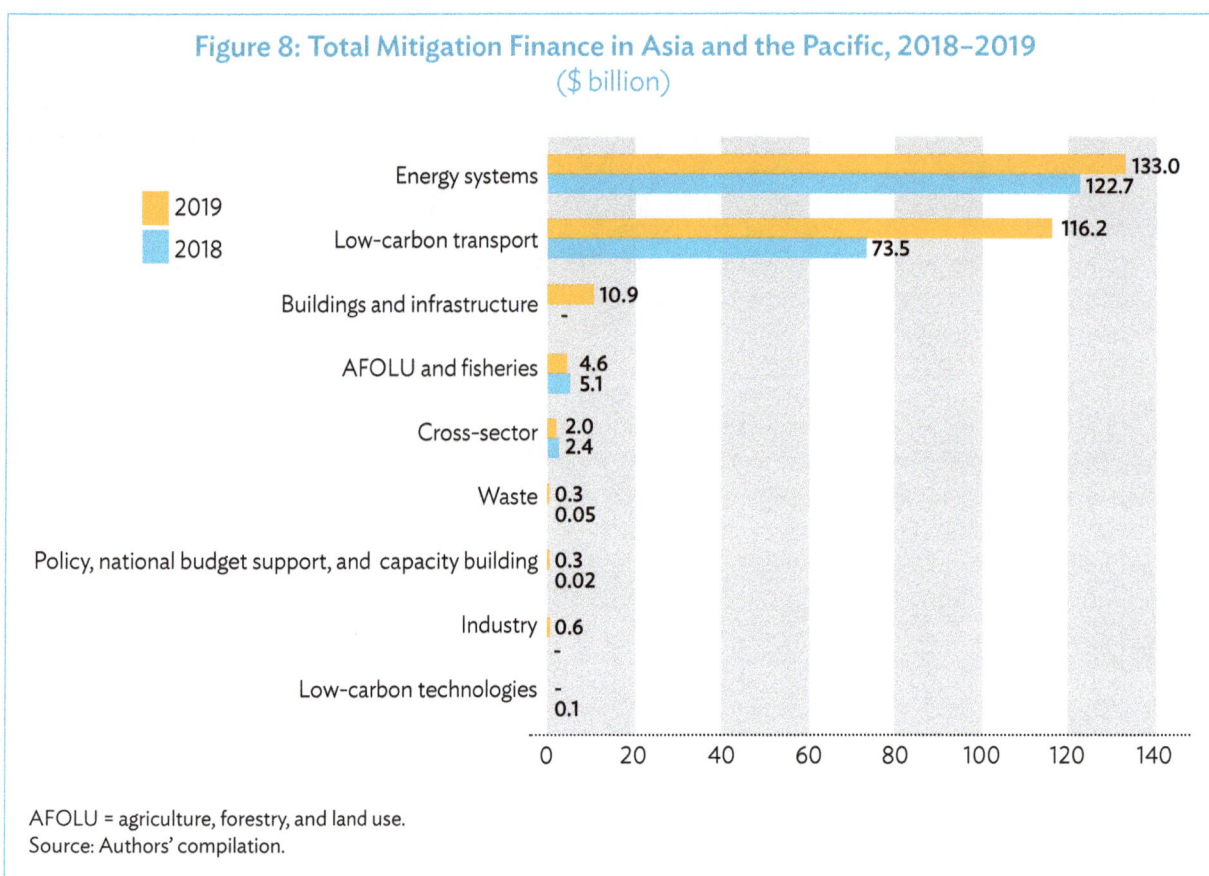

AFOLU = agriculture, forestry, and land use.
Source: Authors' compilation.

Renewable energy projects accounted for the largest portion of mitigation finance in 2018–2019, at $255.6 billion, or 54% of the total. The projects mainly involved solar PV, wind, and hydropower development in the PRC and India. The private sector sustained its commitment to the renewable energy sector. Compared with other climate-related sectors, the energy sector is considered more mature, with proven business models, and more bankable, given the availability of larger-scale projects.

The low-carbon transport sector received the second-largest portion of mitigation finance ($116.2 billion, or 40% of the total). The amount received in 2019 w as 1.5 times the 2018 amount. Most of this finance went to railways, urban transport, and private road transport. Public finance accounted for 75% of total mitigation finance, driven by over several years of government subsidy policies, emphasizing this sector as a key element of the strategy for achieving national emission reduction targets. The remaining 25% came mainly from household spending on private electric vehicles. In supporting the growth of the market for electric vehicles and the potential for decarbonization, governments directed their efforts and finance at capacity building, subsidy programs, and infrastructure development.

The remaining climate finance flowed to (i) AFOLU and fisheries ($9.6 billion, or 2% of the mitigation finance in 2018–2019), mostly for agriculture financing (24% of the total for the sector), and obtained mainly from national and multilateral DFIs; (ii) buildings and infrastructure ($10.9 billion, or 2%), dominated by investments made by governments, corporations, and households in heating, ventilation, and air conditioning; and (iii) cross-sectoral mitigation finance[3] ($5.9 billion, or 1%) for water and wastewater management, industry, low-carbon technology, and capacity building. The industry sector received a smaller portion of mitigation financing during the period ($585 million), for improvements in industrial energy efficiency through the use of more efficient equipment and low-carbon technology, changes in processes, reduction of heat and hot-water loss, increased waste heat recovery, and similar projects. Most mitigation activities in the industry sector pertained to energy efficiency, and were already among those financed in the building and infrastructure sector or the energy sector.

3.2.2 Adaptation Finance

Adaptation finance—8% of total climate finance during the period—increased by 31%, from $17.7 billion in 2018 to $23.1 billion in 2019. Public sources remained the largest contributors, providing $40.6 billion mainly for water and DRM. Only $84 million (0.2% of total adaptation finance in 2018–2019) came from private sources. The growth in adaptation finance was indicative of the level of progress made in climate-resilient development. This was evidenced by the growing public and political awareness of climate impact and risks, resulting in the inclusion of adaptation in climate policies and planning processes in at least 170 countries and many cities (IPCC 2022). The increase in public adaptation finance flows was attributable to the heightened commitments made by DFIs, amounting to $38.6 billion (95% of total adaptation finance). It showed the higher priority given to adaptation in the DFIs' climate finance portfolio, in a positive response to Article 9 of the Paris Agreement, which called for greater balance between mitigation and adaptation finance.

In 2018–2019, water and wastewater management received most of the adaptation finance, at $18.0 billion (44% of total adaptation finance). Governments have evidently stepped up policy measures in this sector, and the developing countries are making earnest efforts to deal with the various water challenges, including flooding, water shortage, and low access to safe water and sanitation. For instance: (i) Indonesia issued Government Regulation Number 27 of 2020, requiring specific treatment for hazardous waste and wastewater; (ii) sustainable water management is among the measures that must be undertaken to improve agroforestry in Viet Nam, according to its Agenda 21; and (iii) the Philippines' Clean Water Act provides for comprehensive water quality management.

The second-highest recipient of adaptation finance was DRM, with $14.4 billion (35% of total adaptation finance), reflecting the growing need in the developing countries to expand investments in early-warning and rapid-response systems for protection against extreme weather events. Weather disasters made 2018 the costliest year on record, with more than $0.5 trillion in global losses (Aon 2019).

The Adaptation Gap Report of the United Nations Environment Programme (UNEP 2021) estimated that annual adaptation costs in developing economies would be in the $140 billion-$300 billion range by 2030. However, according to the report, adaptation finance made up only 8% of climate finance flows in 2018–2019. The low volume of tracked adaptation finance can be attributed to (i) lengthy implementation and long-term planning for adaptation projects; (ii) the nature of adaptation projects, which are often fragmented, small in scale, incremental, and sector specific, making them less financially attractive to private financiers; (iii) the fact that relevant adaptation investments by the domestic public and private sectors are often made as components of larger projects, requiring additional disaggregated information, with a level of detail that is not currently available; and (iv) limitations in existing reporting mechanisms of adaptation finance, such as methodology, framework, and definition constraints, and lack of universally accepted impact metrics (UNFCC 2018; CPI 2019b UNEP 2021; IPCC 2022). Figure 9 shows the sectors that received adaptation finance in 2018–2019, to promote climate-resilient development.

---

[3]   Given the crosscutting nature of adaptation activities, most of them did not fit entirely into a single sectoral category.

Figure 9: Total Adaptation Finance in Asia and the Pacific, 2018–2019
($ billion)

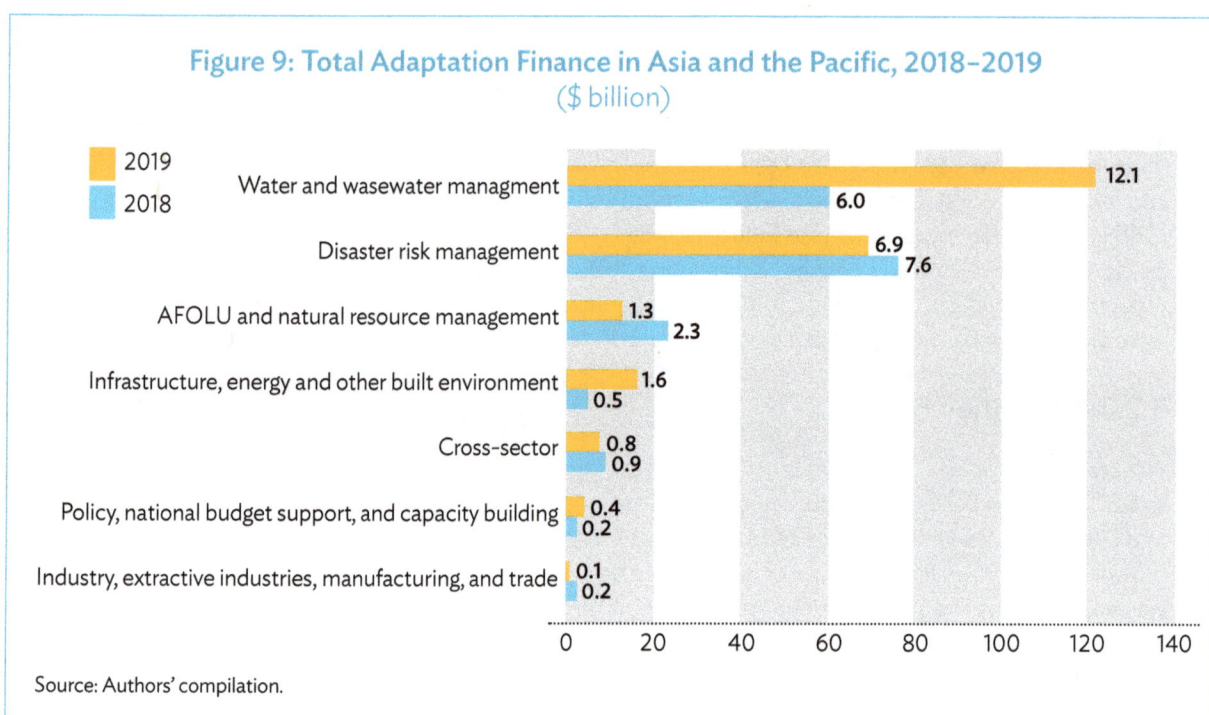

	2019	2018
Water and wasewater managment	12.1	6.0
Disaster risk management	6.9	7.6
AFOLU and natural resource management	1.3	2.3
Infrastructure, energy and other built environment	1.6	0.5
Cross-sector	0.8	0.9
Policy, national budget support, and capacity building	0.4	0.2
Industry, extractive industries, manufacturing, and trade	0.1	0.2

Source: Authors' compilation.

By source, DFIs were the main contributors of adaptation finance. Though, according to the Global Landscape (CPI 2019a), their shar e of adaptation finance was still low ($9.4 billion, 23% of total adaptation finance), MDBs played an enabling role in mobilizing finance by providing grants and concessional loans for climate projects in the developing countries, mainly in the land use, DRM, and water sectors. Since 2019, MDBs have stepped up joint efforts and increased their engagement in financing action on climate and the SDGs. This is recorded by the 2020 Joint Report on Multilateral Development Banks' Climate Finance (AfDB et al. 2021) that highlighted the fact that, of their total climate finance commitment in 2020, 50% w as targeted at climate adaptation by the World Bank.

3.2.3 Dual-Benefit Finance

Climate-related projects and activities contributing to both climate change mitigation and climate change adaptation and meeting the criteria for each category, received the remaining $6.7 billion (1% of total flows) in 2018–2019. An example of dual-benefit project is reforestation and afforestation project preventing erosion in Central Asia and Southeast Asia. These kinds of projects provide significant adaptation benefits, while giving a positive contribution to mitigation (Klein et al., 2007).

3.3 Geographic Flows

Most of the climate finance in Asia and the Pacific in 2018–2019 w ent to East Asia, mainly the PRC (92% of East Asian climate finance flows), followed by South Asia (India for the most part), with 9% of the climate finance (Figure 10), sourced domestically from national DFIs. Figure 10 shows the composition of international and domestic finance in each subregion. Most subregions in Asia and the Pacific, except Southeast Asia, showed an incremental increase in domestic financing allocated to individual countries in 2018–2019. This indicates that local investment is perceived to have less risk because of market familiarity and preference, and highlights the continued importance of strengthening national policies, public finance systems, and regulatory frameworks to encourage investment (CPI 2020).

Climate finance per capita in 2018–2019 (Figure 10) was highest in East Asia ($290), driven by the climate-related expenditures of national governments and private investments in energy systems and electric vehicles. Second highest was climate finance per capita in the Pacific ($114), mainly from international climate funds. In Southeast Asia, however, climate finance remained stagnant during the period, possibly because of budget reallocation by the subregion for economic recovery, particularly for deleveraging and financial risk management to counter the global economic impact of COVID-19.

International finance stayed relatively stable, at $33.9 billion in 2018 and $34.6 billion in 2019. Higher share of international finance was sourced from East Asia and spent mainly in South Asia, the majority of which were directed toward those related to energy systems and low-carbon transport and projects with cross-sectoral impacts.

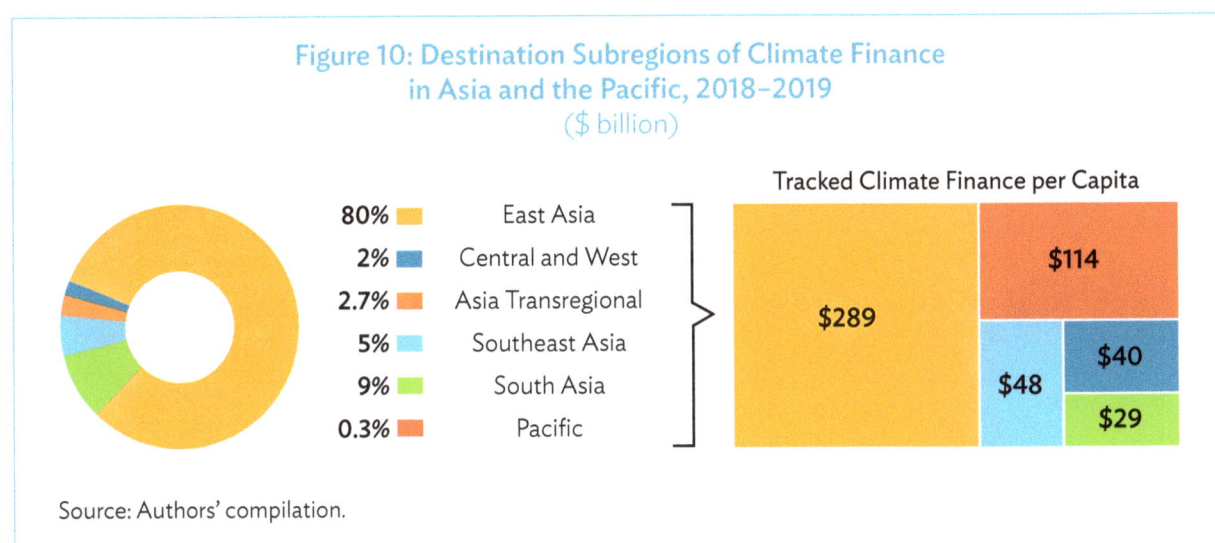

Figure 10: Destination Subregions of Climate Finance in Asia and the Pacific, 2018–2019
($ billion)

80%	East Asia
2%	Central and West
2.7%	Asia Transregional
5%	Southeast Asia
9%	South Asia
0.3%	Pacific

Tracked Climate Finance per Capita

$289 $114 $48 $40 $29

Source: Authors' compilation.

All subregions were highly dependent on public funds (CPI 2019a). There is an evident need to scale up private sector climate finance and to distribute the funds more effectively in the subregions of Asia and the Pacific.

3.4 Financial Instruments

Financial instruments mentioned in CPI (2019a) are debt and equity instruments, at the project level (relying on the project's cash flow for repayment) or on balance sheets (funded with the assets of the recipient institution or entity), and grants. Figure 11 gives a breakdown of the financial instruments used in financing climate projects in Asia and the Pacific in 2018–2019.

Most climate finance in 2018–2019 w as raised through debt financing, which accounted for $365.8 billion annually, or 70% of total flows. Most of the project-level market-rate debt ($190.6 billion, or 52% of total debt in 2018–2019) came from public institutions, primarily national DFIs. Market-rate project debt financing increased by 56%, from $105.0 billion in 2018 to $159.7 billion in 2019. Balance-sheet debt, mostly from capital raised by corporations for renewable energy projects, averaged $38.1 billion annually in 2018–2019, or 21% of total debt. Low-cost project-level debt amounted to $12.5 billion annually, on average, during the period (7% of total debt), 99% of which was provided by public institutions. The overall increase in climate finance over the 2-year period correlates with higher national climate targets, following the Paris Agreement and subsequent net-zero commitments made by countries.

Equity instruments, in the form of direct balance-sheet placements by firms, public entities, and households, made up 24% of total finance in 2018–2019 (80% of total equity finance, or $51.0 billion per year, on average, during the period). The remaining 20% of equity finance, provided at the project level, averaged $12.6 billion per year.

Grants made up 5% of total climate finance in 2018–2019 and the amount remained practically unchanged during the period. Grants averaging $12.5 billion per year were mostly placed by public institutions to finance the transport sector and enabling actions, such as national policies and climate-related projects across a range of sectors.

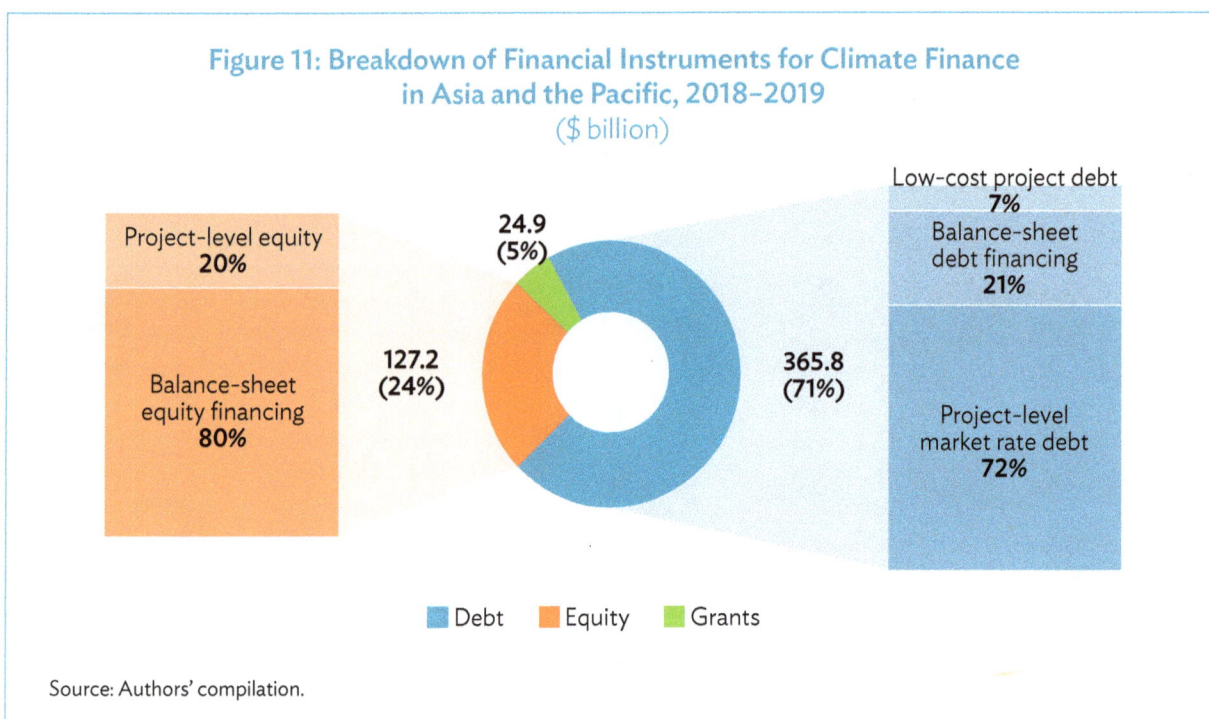

Figure 11: Breakdown of Financial Instruments for Climate Finance in Asia and the Pacific, 2018–2019
($ billion)

Source: Authors' compilation.

3.5 Challenges and opportunities in mobilizing climate finance in Asia and the Pacific

The climate finance landscape of Asia and the Pacific in 2018–2019 is headed in a promising direction, toward low-carbon transition and climate-resilient development, but remains insufficient for achieving the Paris goals. There has been growth in finance for renewable energy, including energy efficiency and low-carbon technology, and government and other public and private sector financiers have provided increased support for low-carbon transport. Adaptation finance has also risen by 30%, as a result of efforts made by both domestic and international sources to rebalance finance flows and redirect the finance particularly to DRM, natural resource management, and coastal protection, given the fact that because of the geographic nature of Asia and the Pacific, most of the population resides in the coastal areas.

However, despite increasing in 2018–2019 to reach a total of $519.9 billion for the period, climate finance in Asia and the Pacific is still not at a sufficient level to contribute to the achievement of the Paris Agreement goal of keeping warming to 1.5°C. Global investment must increase by at least 454%, to $4.1 trillion, to meet the Paris Agreement target (CPI 2021). Asia and the Pacific needs an average annual investment of $1.699 billion up to 2030 (or a total of $16.999 billion over the next decade).

3.5.1 Challenges and Barriers

By presenting the landscape of climate finance in Asia and the Pacific, as well as in each of its five subregions, this report can help improve understanding of the challenges and barriers standing in the way of efforts to close the climate finance gap. **The following key challenges lead to suboptimal climate finance mobilization in Asia and the Pacific:**

- **Insufficient effort to address climate adaptation.** Financing available for adaptation projects is low because these projects are perceived to carry higher investment risk, requiring higher capital up front, and longer-term planning and implementation of projects. Moreover, adaptation projects are usually fragmented, small in scale, incremental, and sector-specific—all potential deterrents to financing, particularly by private investors (IPCC 2022).

  To fully address the climate crisis, cross-boundary strategies, nexus approaches, and more funding must be dedicated to helping countries to achieve climate-resilient development, and both government and the private sector must be committed to making this happen. Adaptation finance is currently provided mostly by the public sector and primarily by DFIs (95% of total adaptation finance), because projects involve long-term planning and implementation. However, financing adaptation projects will require more than these traditional funding sources; it will also call for an appetite for risk that is more likely to be found in the private sector.

  Adaptation finance, according to the Global Landscape (CPI 2019a), incr eased in 2018–2019, but only 0.2% of total adaptation finance during the period came from the private sector. From the private sector standpoint, investing in adaptation should offer various opportunities, such as investing in climate resilience measures to help businesses avoid rising costs due to climate risk, which could have a negative impact on their financial returns (Stenek, Amado, and Greenall 2013); developing new products and services and/or more discrete adaptation investments/products/services to fill market gaps; and achieving cost savings and collaboration across the value chain.

  The private sector holds a key role in the development and implementation of climate projects by virtue of its sector-specific expertise, technology, efficiency, financing, and entrepreneurship. Meanwhile, public financial institutions could provide catalytic financing via blended finance, cofinancing, and the use of risk mitigation instruments, to support private sector participation in adaptation financing.

- **Continued reliance on fossil fuels to drive the economies in all five subregions—Central and West Asia, East Asia, South Asia, Southeast Asia, and the Pacific—**making the low-carbon transition a key challenge. Some countries have already committed themselves to a net-zero target, and most of them are starting to tap into the development of new carbon capture, use, and storage and other promising technologies across all sectors as key strategies. However, a much greater, economy-wide, shift must take place to redirect high-carbon investment into green infrastructure projects, not only in energy systems, but also in other critical sectors, including the agriculture, forestry, and other land use (AFOLU) sector, as well as in transport, water and waste management, and industry.

- **Insufficient and disproportionate climate finance flows, by use and sector, by region, and by source, despite a 31% increase in finance from 2018 to 2019.** The regional landscape shows the unequal distribution of climate finance between mitigation and adaptation. Adaptation finance, averaging $20.4 billion per year in 2018–2019, accounted for only 8% of total climate finance during the period—well below what was needed to respond to the impact of climate change. The UNEP's Adaptation Gap Report (UNEP 2021) estimated annual adaptation costs in the $155–$330 billion range by 2030 in developing economies.

  Climate finance is also unevenly distributed across sectors. In 2018–2019, most of it went to renewable energy and low-carbon transportation. Although many economies in Asia and the Pacific rely on agriculture and have an abundance of forest resources, and despite the relevance of the AFOLU sector to both climate change mitigation and adaptation, climate finance flows to the sector remained stagnant at $7.2 billion per year, or only 3% of total climate finance flows.

  Among the subregions, East Asia was the biggest provider and recipient of climate finance in 2018–2019, receiving 80% of total climate finance in Asia and the Pacific during the period. Nearly all of the tracked finance in East Asia (99%) flowed to the PRC (see Section 4.2: East Asia). South Asia's climate finance flows were the next highest in the region (9% of the total).

  Central and West Asia, Southeast Asia, and the Pacific as a group received less than 8% of total climate finance in Asia and the Pacific. These subregions need more support not only for climate mitigation but, more importantly, for climate adaptation, as they have a combined total of 20 least developed countries and small island developing states, highly vulnerable to the adverse impact of climate change. Central and West Asia is a major fossil fuel producer and user, with an ambitious carbon transition target. Climate finance within the subregion is mostly supported by governments for national strategic projects, and by DFIs for regional projects. The support is sectoral, technologically driven, and often directed toward governments, causing unequal and insufficient funding distribution by bilateral and multilateral funders. This, along with a lack of regional support, has led to unequal climate action.

  The Pacific, for its part, is heavily exposed to the adverse impact of climate change; adaptation effort is therefore critical, but costs are significant and fiscal space is limited. Public sector investment costs for adaptation are disproportionately high in Pacific Island countries because of their expensive coastal protection infrastructure needs. Average investment needs for the Pacific, mainly for adaptation measures, are estimated at $540 million annually.

  With respect to source, the public sector accounted for 68% of total finance flows in 2018–2019, indicating that climate projects rely heavily on public funds, while private investments, at 32%, are lagging behind. Most subregions in Asia and the Pacific depend on public sources of climate finance—domestic and international—mainly from DFIs (CPI 2019a). Only South Asia can access both public and private finance in almost equal proportions. Following South Asia's pathway is recommended, as the subregion is able to better leverage and optimize existing public finance to attract and mobilize private finance.

  Collective effort is pivotal in coming up with the high financing needed to fulfill climate pledges; public financing alone is unlikely to mobilize these investments. But private investors, such as financial institutions, still shy away from investing in the most impactful projects, and countries most vulnerable to climate change are unable to attract available funding. This mismatch between supply and demand of climate finance is a major barrier to reaching a sufficient level of investment in the sector, region, or country that needs it most.

- **Limited access to long-term finance, especially for small-scale climate projects, jeopardizing the ability to attract sufficient investment to the sector, region, or country where it is most needed.** As climate finance supplier, developed countries missed the target of delivering $100 billion in climate finance a year to developing countries by 2020, but the 2021 United Nations Climate Change Conference (COP26), in a resolution, reiterated that this target would be met by 2023 (OECD 2021).

A gap exists between the ambitions of financial institutions to invest in the most impactful projects and the ability of the country's most vulnerable to climate change to attract available funding. The scale of projects affects the willingness of financial institutions to consider providing finance—the smaller the scale, the higher the cost stemming from economies of scale in due diligence. Many climate-related projects require high cost of capital and longer-tenor financing in order for the benefits and return on investment to be realized. However, long-term financing is often difficult and more expensive to obtain in many least-developed countries (LDCs). This could be due in part to a lack of capital markets or regulatory restrictions on long-term bank lending.[4]

- **Gaps in institutional capacity and arrangements for access to climate finance.** A lack of strong institutional capacity poses challenges in accessing climate finance. The institutional architecture of climate finance, including guidance on how it should be led, arranged, and coordinated, is still developing in the developing countries. Weak leadership or coordination could result in the inefficient use of already inadequate climate finance, and in misalignment between donor interventions, development efforts, and government policies (Amerasinghe et al. 2017). The lack of a common vision and the varying climate finance perspectives among government officials, political authorities, and other stakeholders could also hinder effective interaction between private financiers, international donors, and domestic bureaucracies (Clar 2019).

  Moreover, there is an insufficiency of available and accessible sources of finance. Most climate finance is raised through debt instruments, which pose difficult repayment obligations for developing countries, thus limiting their capacity to access finance and scale it up. Grants, on the other hand, account for only 5% of climate finance in Asia and the Pacific, and need to be increased. Without additional grant-based access, meeting the climate finance requirements will be a challenge.

Access to finance could also be impeded by the low readiness of recipients, which may be due to gaps in meeting the funding and safeguard requirements of international donors and agencies. The Global Landscape (CPI 2019a) not es that the role of international finance is still limited, despite the funding pledges or commitments that have been made. It is therefore important to ensure not only the readiness and capacity of recipients, but also the accessibility of fund sources.

Many countries need technical support in applying for international grants and financial assistance, including support in preparing the application documents. For instance, within the GCF accreditation program, the Pacific has been using the readiness programs and the Simplified Approval Process modality to identify remaining gaps in documentation, capacity, and policies that must be addressed to gain access to international financing (IMF 2021b). Indonesia, through the Fiscal Policy Agency of the Ministry of Finance, as the National Designated Authority of the GCF, organized a forum for all participating climate finance focal points in 2021. The forum was intended to strengthen the dissemination of information on the key characteristics of each international funding institution, the financing instruments, and the targeted sectors, to help the country prepare application documents for international climate financing. Increased capacity through information sharing would improve the efficiency of climate finance, and avoid overlap in funding in similar projects or programs (Ministry of Finance, Indonesia, 2021).

Moreover, access to adaptation finance is very competitive and most funding goes to larger Asian countries, where institutional capacity tends to be greater. A clear understanding of internationally recognized safeguards for various financing modalities and climate-related projects would improve capacity and readiness for climate finance among countries and subregions in Asia and the Pacific, particularly those that rely heavily on international assistance, such as the Pacific (see Fiji case study in Section 4.5.4). Better capacity will make access to climate finance sources more likely.

---

4   Climate-related projects are perceived to carry high risk because of lack of familiarity with the various low-carbon technologies, and the projects' high capital requirement and longer payback period. Moreover, economic gowth in developing countries creates competing investment needs, leading to higher interest rates and costlier funding.

- **Capacity gaps in climate finance tracking and reporting and lack of transparency and disclosure, which may result in incomplete assessment of climate finance effectiveness and impact.** Impact assessment helps policy makers determine the strategic direction for national climate policy to enhance the mobilization of funds. Gaps in climate finance data keep the government and key stakeholders from gaining a clearer and more complete perspective on underserved regions, countries, or sectors, and constrain efforts to capture more granular information because of definitional issues and unsystematized information (GFLAC and UNDP 2018).

The Global Landscape (CPI 2019a) t akes note of challenges in obtaining data on both public and private climate finance. There is limited information on domestic public climate finance in public budgets dedicated to domestic climate action. While several countries track climate finance, institutional limitations prevent a full accounting of those public budgets (CPI 2021). Some countries like Bangladesh, India, and Indonesia are better at tracking climate action information on public budgets with the help of the Climate Budget Tagging tool,[5] but this mechanism is still limited to tracking national budgets; it does not fully cover the tagging of expenditure from state-owned enterprises (SOEs) or other government agencies, and does not yet consider the mapping of private sector investments. These limitations may result in an information gap in climate finance tracking and reporting.

There is also a lack of transparency in the private sector, despite the existence of the industry-based Task Force on Climate-Related Financial Disclosures (TCFD). Data on private investment in energy efficiency, low-carbon transport, and land use are still largely unavailable for confidentiality reasons. Often, the relevant investments form part of larger projects, which require additional voluntary reporting and disclosure by private stakeholders. Disclosure by the private sector has so far been limited, however, constraining tracking at the project level.

Tracking and reporting of adaptation finance, which has been shown to lag significantly behind mitigation finance (CPI 2019a) also faces key barriers. These include (i) the lack of universally accepted impact metrics for defining adaptation finance; (ii) limitations in adaptation finance accounting methodology; and (iii) constraints on the definition of adaptation-relevant activities (UNFCCC 2018; CPI 2019b).

Moreover, for adaptation finance to be effective, it must be consistent with climate-resilient pathways and not just represent an arbitrary improvement over business as usual. But to assess consistency, there must be reporting on progress against benchmarks or standards, and currently disclosed data provide insufficient details on this matter. Deficiencies in disclosure and project-level data pose financial, institutional, and coordination constraints on the tracking and monitoring of adaptation and private finance in some countries. These limitations lead to under-tracking and underreporting of the overall level of climate finance.

What is more, attracting private sector investors demands institutional capacity to develop a robust proof of concept, in order to demonstrate that the projects will not only reduce the severity of climate change and support climate-resilient development but will also deliver a return on investment.

---

[5]   Climate Budget Tagging (CBT) is a tool for monitoring and tracking climate-related expenditures in the national budget system.

3.5.2 Challenges caused by the COVID-19 Pandemic

Aside from the above key challenges, the fallout from the COVID-19 pandemic laid bare the structural vulnerabilities affecting climate finance flows in 2020, especially in developing countries.

Levels of climate finance in 2020 were influenced by the actual levels of public finance provided and the extent to which private finance could be mobilized through public interventions. Globally, total climate finance has steadily increased over the last decade, reaching $632 billion in 2019–2020, but flows have slowed down in the last few years, particularly in 2020, when COVID-19 broke out (CPI 2021). Climate finance flows increased by only 10% per year in 2017–2018 and 2019–2020, well below the increase of more than 24% recorded in previous periods (CPI 2021).

The COVID-19 pandemic has put much pressure on the economy of Asia and the Pacific and contributed to delays in the implementation of climate actions and NDCs. In 2020, the renewables sector struggled along with most other economic sectors as governments imposed lockdowns and mobility restrictions, bringing the ongoing renewable energy projects to an almost complete halt (IESR 2021). In the agriculture and fisheries sector, the mobility restrictions, as well as reduced purchasing power, disrupted food demand, supply, and security. Among the most vulnerable population groups, the impact was even greater (OECD 2022).

Some recovery measures were introduced in response to the pandemic. Among these were fiscal incentives and policy actions integrating low-carbon and climate-resilient economic development. Economic stimulus packages were also implemented. For instance, India, Indonesia, and the Philippines as a group have announced a total of $424.6 billion in economic recovery packages since the start of the pandemic in February 2020 (Aylward-Mills et al. 2021). However, the "green" portion of the measures was limited and was directed mostly at the energy and transport sectors. Opportunities in other key sectors, such as agriculture and forestry, waste management and recycling, and climate change adaptation, were missed (OECD 2022).

The Greenness of Stimulus Index developed by Vivid Economics assessed the sustainability implications of the fiscal stimulus packages on the countries and suggested that they were not doing enough to incorporate climate considerations into their fiscal stimulus response. Increasing restrictions on monetary and fiscal space, undermining the ability of the countries to finance mitigation and adaption measures, could be responsible (Vivid Economics and Finance for Biodiversity Initiative 2021; Hourcade et al. 2021).

3.5.3 Opportunities and Recommendations

Addressing the foregoing challenges requires collective effort and coordination among governments, funding institutions, the private sector, and other key stakeholders, to enhance the flows and impact of climate finance. To accelerate and scale up climate finance in Asia and the Pacific, these stakeholders must do the following:

- **Ensure that climate finance is available, sufficient, and accessible, and is targeted at underserved subregions, countries, and sectors with the most impact on achieving NDC targets, by**
  » streamlining the coordination of the international and national public and private sectors in carrying out their climate finance roles and responsibilities (see Box 3 on climate finance coordination in the Kyrgyz Republic);
  » redirecting the regulatory framework, through the mainstreaming of climate targets into national planning and policy, the definition of an oversight mechanism among government agencies, and other means;
  » strengthening the government's policy framework to mainstream climate finance into national planning;
  » leveraging the government's fiscal capacity, through subsidies, tax incentives, public–private partnerships (PPPs), and other measures, to attract private investors by mitigating the financial risks, and influencing financial regulations to crowd in private finance for climate action (e.g., regulations classifying climate-related activities and placing a portion of the banks' loan portfolios in climate projects);

» ensuring policy coherence across sectors;

» sustaining the catalytic role of governments and MDBs through blended finance, cofinancing, and scaled-up risk management instruments; and

» ensuring the accessibility of climate finance, by prioritizing grants and concessional funding, particularly for the countries and sectors that need financial support the most.

- **Improve understanding of climate finance effectiveness and impact,** as this would enhance the capacity of developing countries to use and disburse finance to achieve the highest value for every dollar flow, possibly leading to the upscaling of climate projects and finance. There is also an apparent opportunity to close the knowledge gap by sharing lessons from countries that have had more success in (i) mobilizing finance by having a national strategy, as well as national mitigation and adaptation policies and plans aligned with NDC priorities; and (ii) meeting the funding requirements of international donors or agencies (see Box 7 on the subregional learning and sharing effort to close the knowledge and capacity gap under the Climate Finance Readiness for the Pacific Project of the Pacific Islands Forum Secretariat).

- **Overcome barriers to long-term financing.** Some developing countries have set an example:

  » Accessing low-cost debt through a national development bank. The China Development Bank provided $80 billion in low-cost debt for renewable energy projects, at a time when most solar projects and over five-sixths of wind projects were built and owned by SOEs (by mid-2012). The collaboration between the national development bank and SOEs provided subsidized low-cost debt for low-carbon and climate-resilient development at scale.

  » Introducing energy-sector initiatives that replaced subsidies with feed-in-tariffs or power purchase agreements, to reduce other costs to the government, as was done in India and Indonesia (UNESCAP 2016).

- **Enhance transparency and capacity for climate finance tracking and reporting, by**

  » continuing to develop a methodology and framework for climate finance tracking by the national government;

  » enhancing disclosure across financial systems, covering commercial financial institutions and other related stakeholders that invest in climate-related activities, and taking the initiative to measure, disclose, manage, and mitigate climate risks in the private sector, e.g., compliance by commercial financial institutions with the recommendation of the Task Force on Climate-Related Financial Disclosures (TCFD);

  » continuously improving methodologies to fill gaps in private investment and adaptation finance data (e.g., easing confidentiality restrictions and addressing the absence of universally accepted impact metrics) and enable full accounting and tracking of finance; and

  » improving access to and mobilization of global international climate initiatives and finance, by establishing a robust institutional framework with technical guidelines to meet the high level of safeguards imposed by international climate finance institutions, and by developing a consistent system for tracking finance and monitoring the progress of adaption measures. Climate risk management should also become mandatory.

- **Enhance the capacity of governments to plan and mobilize resources on the basis of climate finance data, e.g., by identifying gaps in finance, for better alignment with climate policy objectives.** Comprehensive information from the climate finance database can induce a large volume of finance, on the assumption that key stakeholders respond rationally to information on climate finance data (quantitative) and policy signals (qualitative) to redirect investment flows, domestic and international, to targeted subregions, countries, and sectors (quantitative) and policy signals (qualitative) to redirect investment flows, domestic and international, to targeted subregions, countries, and sectors.

Data limitations have laid bare the gaps in climate finance tracking and reporting; the granular level of climate finance could therefore be under-tracked and underreported. More efforts are needed to capture the significant potential for tracking climate finance from the private sector and for enhancing domestic public finance methodology, such as: (i) defining key services and technologies, and working with key data providers across a variety of stakeholders to improve data quality; (ii) optimizing finance for strategic climate projects; and (iii) sharing lessons learned from countries that have succeeded in enhancing transparency and improving their data tracking for better alignment of investments with resources. Box 2 sets out some examples of efforts taken by developing countries to narrow the data gap.

Box 2: Narrowing the Data Gap—Efforts to Track Private Investment and Domestic National Climate Finance in Asia and the Pacific

Publicly available data on adaptation, private investment, and domestic public finance still lag behind in landscape assessment. Some efforts have been made to identify private finance. For instance, Mongolia formed the Green Taxonomy Committee in 2018 to harmonize the definition of climate finance and clarify eligible green investment activities. Since then, the Central Bank of Mongolia has started compiling statistics on green loans. These loans currently account for only about 2% of its total loan portfolio, highlighting the potential for increasing green and sustainable financing from the private sector (see East Asia, Mongolia case study in Section 4.2.4).

The gaps in tracking of domestic public finance have also been addressed in some countries. Indonesia, for instance, tracked domestic public finance by using the Climate Budget Tagging tool, and its upcoming Climate Fiscal Framework (CFF) projects a potentially large financial supply gap in the $356–$375 billion range, providing more transparent information on the achievement of its climate targets in 2020–2060 (see Southeast Asia, Indonesia case study in Section 4.4.4). Bangladesh, for its part, enhanced its public finance methodology to include adaptation finance (see South Asia, Bangladesh case study in Section 4.3.4).

4 Subregional Landscape Assessment

4.1 Central and West Asia

Armenia, Azerbaijan, Georgia, Kazakhstan, the Kyrgyz Republic, Pakistan, Tajikistan, Turkmenistan, and Uzbekistan are the Central and West Asian countries included in this report.

The subregion covers about 5.9 million square kilometers, and has a population of around 313 million (2021), around 5% of the world population. The subregion's GDP growth rate increased from 3.50% in 2015 to 4.47% in 2018, bringing the average GDP to around 3.82% during the period (World Bank 2020). The increase in GDP was driven by reliance on fossil fuel resources. Azerbaijan, Kazakhstan, and Uzbekistan produce fossil fuel for domestic use and export, and engage in fossil fuel–fired power generation. These countries are dominant sources of GHG emissions in the subregion.

4.1.1 Background of the Subregion

As the center of the world's oil and gas production and reserves, the Central and West Asian economies still depend on fossil fuel resources for energy production and infrastructure development, making a shift to low-carbon growth more difficult (ADB 2012). The subregion, given its topography, is also highly vulnerable to climate-related risks. For instance, accelerated glacial melt increases the risk of flooding and riverine erosion, thus adversely affecting agriculture production. Once the glaciers retreat, and as rainfall patterns continue to change, drought is likely to occur, threatening energy generation and water supply.

Heavy reliance on fossil fuel increases the need to adopt low-carbon transition strategies. Cost-effective clean energy technologies, energy efficiency innovations, and low-carbon transport can play a key role in achieving the subregion's climate goals and decarbonization initiative. Table 3 summarizes the climate change program priorities of countries in the subregion.

Some countries have developed their own climate policies and targets. For instance:

- The Kyrgyz Republic, which has a high-level Coordinating Commission on Green Economy Development and Climate Change, submitted its updated NDC in 2021, increasing its climate commitments for 2030. The updated NDC clearly states the country's commitment to reduce GHG emissions by 15.97% under the "business as usual" (BAU) scenario, and by 43.6 2% with international support, despite being a relatively low emitter, compared with other countries in the subregion.

- Azerbaijan and Uzbekistan, top suppliers of energy sourced from natural gas in the subregion, are speeding up the transition process by developing a solar road map and a state program for hydropower development to meet their renewable energy targets.

- Kazakhstan, the largest country and top coal producer in Central and West Asia, leads in international climate financing in the subregion and has identified adaptation priorities and ambitious mitigation measures for clean energy transition and energy efficiency (World Bank 2020).

Table 3: Snapshot of Climate Change Priorities in Central and West Asia, 2018–2019

Country	tCO$_2$e Per Capita in 2020	Net-Zero Target (Year)	LTS/LT Submission	NDC Priority Sectors	NDC Target	Finance Needs	Domestic Public Expenditure on Climate as a Share of National Budget
Armenia	1.98	Not yet announced	2050 mitigation goal of reducing GHG emissions to at most 2.07 tCO$_2$e per capita	Energy, transport, waste, AFOLU (including fisheries), adaptation (natural ecosystem, water resources, built infrastructure)	Armenia's first NDC (updated submission in 2021) 40% reduction from 1990 emission levels by 2030	N/A; under preparation as part of National NDC Implementation Plan	3.2% on average in 2017–2019
Azerbaijan	3.36	Not yet announced	Not yet submitted	Energy, transport, AFOLU, waste	Azerbaijan's first NDC, submitted in 2017 as Intended NDC 35% GHG emission reduction compared with 1990 base year by 2030	N/A	4.4% in 2020: 3.4% for agriculture and 1.0% for environmental protection
Georgia	2.68	Not yet announced	Not yet submitted	Transport, buildings, energy, industry, waste, AFOLU, adaptation (ecosystem and natural resources, water, and biodiversity)	Georgia's first NDC (updated submission in 2021) Unconditional: 35% GHG emission reduction by 2030, compared with 1990 base year Conditional: 50%–57% GHG emission reduction by 2030	N/A	N/A
Kazakhstan	14.2	2060	Not yet submitted	Energy, agriculture, waste, land use, land-use change, and forestry	Kazakhstan's first NDC, submitted in 2016 as Intended NDC Unconditional: 15% GHG emission reduction by 2030, compared with 1990 base year Conditional: 25% GHG emission reduction by 2030, compared with 1990 base year	N/A	N/A

Continued on next page

Table 3 continued

Country	tCO$_2$e Per Capita in 2020	Net-Zero Target (Year)	LTS/LT Submission	NDC Priority Sectors	NDC Target	Finance Needs	Domestic Public Expenditure on Climate as a Share of National Budget
Kyrgyz Republic	1.82	2050	Not yet submitted	Energy, transport, AFOLU, adaptation (water, biodiversity, and cross-sectoral, including climate-resilient areas and green cities)	Kyrgyz Republic's first NDC (updated submission in 2021) Unconditional: GHG reduction of 16.62% by 2025 and 15.97% by 2030, under BAU scenario Conditional: GHG reduction of 36.61% by 2025 and 43.62% by 2030 under BAU scenario	Conditional: $10 billion (2020–2030), consisting of mitigation finance of $7.2 billion and adaptation finance of $2.8 billion	0.6% on average in 2017–2019
Pakistan	1.04	2050	Not yet submitted	Energy, transportation, land-use change, and forestry, including new sectors such as blue economy, air pollution, and carbon market	Pakistan's first NDC (updated submission in 2021) Unconditional: GHG reduction of 15% by 2030 Conditional: GHG reduction of 35% by 2030	Unconditional: $101 billion (2020–2030) Conditional: $166 billion (2020–2030)	6.7% in 2011–2012; 8.4% in 2014–2015
Tajikistan	0.95	2050	Not yet submitted	Agriculture, energy, forestry and biodiversity, industry and construction, transport, and infrastructure	Tajikistan's first NDC (updated submission in 2021) Unconditional: not to exceed 60%–70% of 1990 GHG emissions by 2030 Conditional: not to exceed 50%–60% of 1990 GHG emissions by 2030, subject to international funding and technology transfer	$10 billion (2020–2030)	N/A

Continued on next page

Table 3 continued

Country	tCO$_2$e Per Capita in 2020	Net-Zero Target (Year)	LTS/LT Submission	NDC Priority Sectors	NDC Target	Finance Needs	Domestic Public Expenditure on Climate as a Share of National Budget
Turkmenistan	13.3	2050	Not yet submitted	Energy, industry, agriculture, waste	Turkmenistan's first NDC (submitted in 2016 as Intended NDC) Contribution toward GHG emission reduction and prevention of an increase of more than 2°C in the global average temperature	N/A	N/A
Uzbekistan	2.7	2050	Not yet submitted	Energy, transportation, agriculture, adaptation	Uzbekistan's first NDC (Updated Submission in 2021) Reduction in GHG emissions per unit of GDP, and 35% reduction in the 2010 level by 2030 (instead of the 10% provided for in NDC1)	N/A	N/A

AFOLU = agriculture, forestry, and land use; BAU = business as usual; GHG = greenhouse gas; LTS/LT = long-term strategy/long term; NDC = Nationally Determined Contribution; tCO2e = metric tons of carbon dioxide equivalent.

Note: N/A = data not available. In this table's last column, the reference is to the absence of disclosed information on domestic public expenditure on climate-related activities and projects as a share of the national budget.

Sources: Joint Research Centre, European Commission (2020); United Nations Framework Convention on Climate Change (UNFCCC) NDC Registry.

4.1.1 Subregional Landscape and Key Trends

Central and West Asia received $12.4 billion in climate finance in 2018–2019, or only 2% of the climate finance total for Asia and the Pacific during the period. Pakistan was the destination for most of the finance, totaling $5.6 billion (45% of total flows in this subregion), followed by Uzbekistan, with $2.5 billion (21% of the subregion's climate finance), and Kazakhstan, with $2.0 billion (16%).

More than half of the subregion's climate projects received public funding, totaling $7.8 billion (64%), primarily for mitigation (74%). Based on NDCs of Central and West Asia, total climate investment needs up to 2030 have been estimated at $186 billion, mainly for mitigation measures, indicating the necessity of accelerating adaptation financing, especially given the subregion's climate vulnerability.

Financing sources. Public finance accounted for 64% of climate finance in the subregion in 2018–2019, increasing from $3.1 billion in 2018 to $4.8 billion in 2019. DFIs provided most of this financing—$6.7 billion, or 85% of the subregion's public finance total, comprising $5.9 billion (87%) from multilateral DFIs, $660 million (9%) from bilateral DFIs, and $153 million (2%) from national DFIs.

The Global Landscape (2019a) c aptured the shift in financing trend from AFOLU and fisheries, and building and infrastructure, to energy and low-carbon transport. The government budget and agencies increased their share of financing by 72%, from $289 million in 2018 to $530 million in 2019 (10% of the subregion's public finance), chiefly as a result of a more ambitious national commitment to meeting climate targets for emission reduction and clean energy transition. Multilateral climate funds contributed stable financing, providing $159 million in 2018 and $142 million in 2019. The Global Environment Facility (GEF) and the GCF were the main sources of support for regional climate actions. Their financing was mostly directed at energy transformation and hydropower development. Besides mitigation projects, adaptation programs, such as the Aral Sea Basin Program and its national components in Tajikistan and Uzbekistan, also received GCF support (World Bank 2020).

Sectors financed. Of the total climate finance in Central and West Asia in 2018–2019, 74% was for mitigation finance, most of it for the energy sector. This was an apparent response to the subregion's significant need for support, and efforts made, in energy transformation, security, and resilience. Adaptation finance, 20% of the subregional total, went mainly to agriculture and DRM projects, such as hydrometeorology and disaster risk reduction, to improve weather forecasting and flood warning systems in the Kyrgyz Republic and Tajikistan, with World Bank assistance.

The remaining 6% of the subregion's climate finance was for dual-benefit projects aimed at climate-related outcomes. Among these projects were those that involved policy making and technical assistance to enhance the subregion's capacity and preparedness to respond to the impact of climate change, e.g., GIZ-supported climate impact analysis and science–policy links (World Bank 2020).

Figure 12 breaks down the uses of climate finance in the Central and West Asia subregion in 2018–2019.

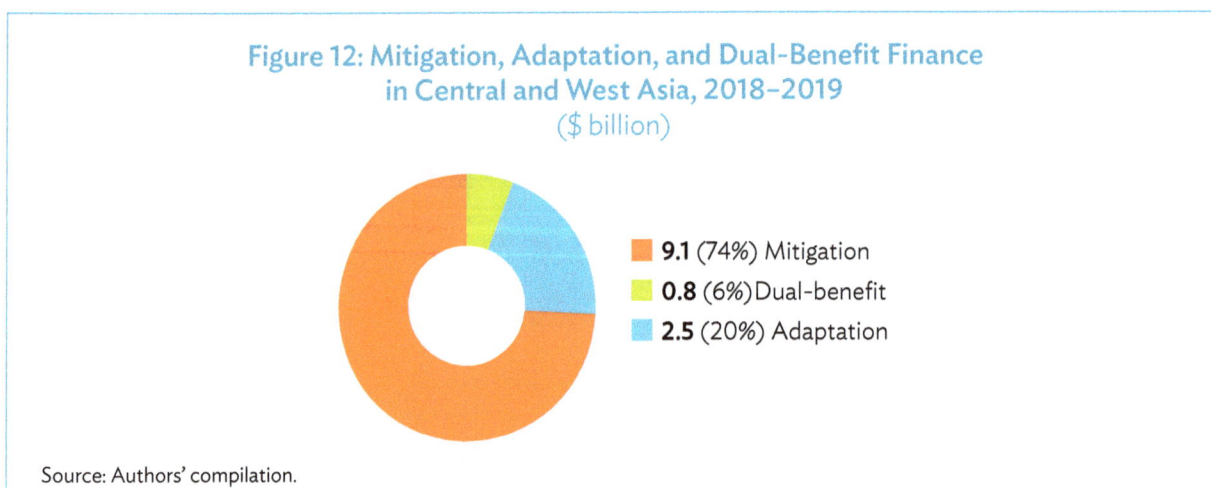

Figure 12: Mitigation, Adaptation, and Dual-Benefit Finance in Central and West Asia, 2018–2019
($ billion)

- **9.1** (74%) Mitigation
- **0.8** (6%) Dual-benefit
- **2.5** (20%) Adaptation

Source: Authors' compilation.

Financing instruments. Debt was a key financing instrument in 2018–2019, accounting for $7.5 billion, or 61% of the subregion's climate finance during the period. Project-level debt, made available, for the most part, by multilateral DFIs for energy and low-carbon transport projects, was mainly provided at market rates ($4.9 billion), attracting the private sector. Low-cost project-level debt ($1.9 billion) supplied by the public sector, on the other hand, supported the subregion's more ambitious climate goals, based on the latest NDC submission in 2021. Balanc e-sheet debt was provided by commercial institutions for renewable energy projects ($648 million).

Grants made up 9% of total climate finance in the subregion during the period ($1.1 billion), increasing by 61% from $454 million in 2018 to $732 million in 2019. Grants, mostly from public institutions, financed energy transition in the transport sector, and supported national policies and adaptation projects. Equity instruments (30% of total climate finance in Central and West Asia in 2018–2019) provided financing through direct balance-sheet placement ($3.0 billion, or 71% of total equity instruments). Project-level equity financing from corporations and public entities amounted to $603 million, or 29% of total equity instruments.

Figure 13 classifies climate finance in Central and West Asia in 2018–2019 ac cording to the instruments used in the subregion.

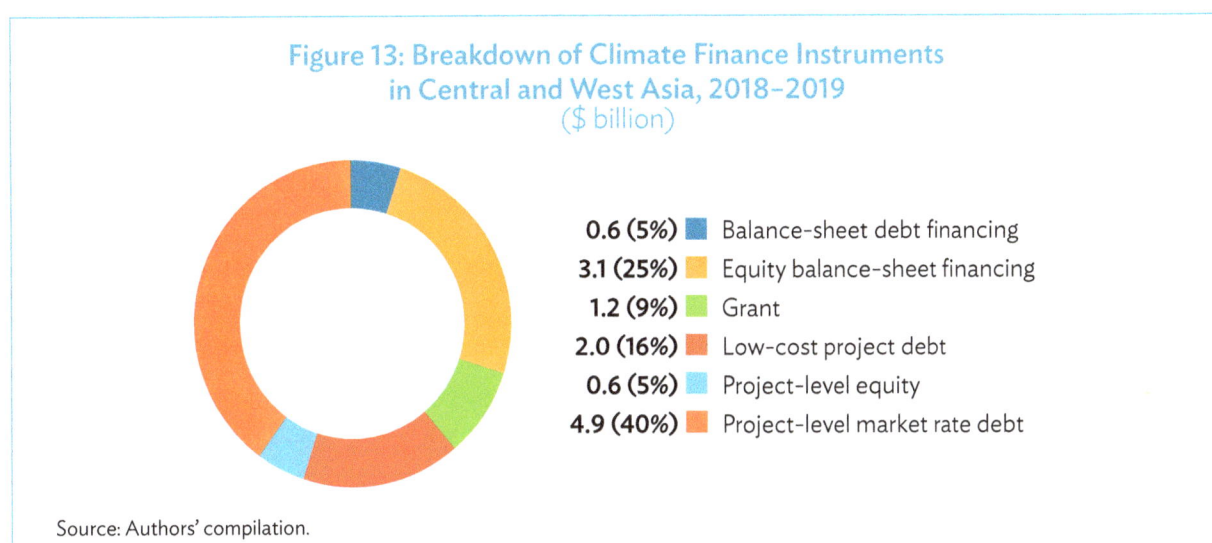

Figure 13: Breakdown of Climate Finance Instruments in Central and West Asia, 2018–2019
($ billion)

0.6 (5%)	Balance-sheet debt financing
3.1 (25%)	Equity balance-sheet financing
1.2 (9%)	Grant
2.0 (16%)	Low-cost project debt
0.6 (5%)	Project-level equity
4.9 (40%)	Project-level market rate debt

Source: Authors' compilation.

Impact of COVID-19 on climate finance flow. The pandemic resulted in a negative GDP growth rate of –2.8% in 2020. In Central and West Asia, mobility restrictions reduced energy demand and caused uncertainty in the energy sector, adversely affecting countries whose economies relied on fossil fuels, such as Kazakhstan and Turkmenistan (IEA 2020).

In climate adaptation, the pandemic deepened existing vulnerabilities and challenges in disaster risk management (DRM). The subregion was able to draw support for climate adaptation from the United Nations Office for Disaster Risk Reduction (UNDDR) in the form of capacity building to develop and strengthen coordination in disaster risk reduction from the national to the subregional level (UNDDR 2022).

Gap analysis. Central and West Asia faced challenges in shifting from its reliance on fossil fuels, given their abundance and the economic benefits associated with producing and consuming the fuels. However, efforts have been made: investments in climate mitigation projects in the energy, transport, urban, and other sectors, mainly from international financing sources (67% of total climate finance in the subregion in 2018–2019), increased in 2018–2019. This implies that the region has access to funds and the potential to scale up its climate financing, and particularly to redirect it toward adaptation projects.

To narrow the gap in adaptation finance, the subregion has launched multicountry programs providing climate benefits to the subregion, such as hydrometeorology services, DRM, afforestation, and water management. In addition, the European Union–Central Asia Environment, Climate Change and Water Cooperation (WECOOP) program has produced a guide for investors on the preparation of investment projects in the environment, climate change, and water management in Central and West Asia, particularly those promoting energy efficiency, clean energy, and green development (World Bank 2020).

4.1.3 Challenges and Opportunities

This subregion has prioritized renewable energy, energy efficiency, and adaptation projects such as climate-resilient water supply, agriculture, and DRM, given its geographic location (the presence of glaciers, mountains, and river basins) and carbon-intensive economies (growing populations and economic dependence on abundant fossil fuels as primary energy source). Climate finance mobilization must therefore be targeted at projects with the most impact on emission reduction and resilience to climate change. However, of the total tracked finance in 2018–2019, only 2% went into climate action. Cheap and abundant supply of fossil fuels, poor local renewable energy resources, and unfavorable investment environments for international financiers, in combination, have limited the mobilization of climate financing in the subregion.

The subregion has nonetheless received a wide variety of climate financing. For example, Tajikistan was the top recipient of international grant funding, often blended with soft loans, in 2018–2019, while Kazakhstan led in loan-based climate financing, with the private sector playing a significant role in the subregion (World Bank 2020).

Detailed information on climate investment in the subregion, such as domestic public and private finance, is not fully available, despite an increase in the amount of climate finance. Central and West Asian countries report to the UNFCCC only the financing they receive from global climate funds, and not the full range of their climate-related projects. Besides, many renewable energy projects (e.g., hydropower, solar, and wind) and energy-efficient buildings are financed mostly from the government budget and by private investors, who may not report their climate projects. Moreover, some projects cofinanced by the public and private sectors lack climate finance coordination; unclear roles and responsibilities in measurement, reporting, and verification (MRV) could result in underreporting of climate-related investments. The tracking of climate finance has become more challenging as a result.

The governments of the Central and West Asian countries have opportunities to mainstream and promote climate finance reporting to align national policy actions with climate goals, through the following:

- Harmonization of climate finance data to make more visible the correlation between climate investments and emission reduction outcomes. Enhanced climate finance coordination and transparency could improve the subregion's credibility and accountability when accessing international climate funding.

- Better understanding of climate finance through MRV to help governments (i) direct fiscal stimulus measures to low-carbon and underfunded sectors, and (ii) better mobilize finance for disaster risk response and other adaptation efforts, especially to support post-COVID recovery.

- Encouragement of private sector initiatives promoting energy transformation and climate-resilient development. Centralized climate finance data would enable the private sector to support climate actions, such as divestment from high-emitting sectors (e.g., coal and natural gas) in favor of low-carbon sectors (e.g., hydropower, solar, and other sources of renewable energy).

- Quantitative-based tracking, synthesizing the nature, trend, flow, and source of climate finance vs. climate target vs. climate outcome, in order to (i) introduce protective measures, such as dam safety improvements and prevention and nature-based solutions; (ii) identify the investment needed to meet climate targets; and (iii) put in place incentive mechanisms to bridge investment gaps and leverage private finance.

- Cooperation among countries in the subregion in promoting green investment and attracting private sector participation. Central and West Asia faces circular economy barriers, such as wide use of fossil fuels, water shortage, and lack of effective waste management, underscoring the importance of strategies for attracting sufficient funding and directing it toward sustainable development in the subregion. The European

Union established its WECOOP subregional cooperation program to help Central and West Asia move closer toward a circular economy by enhancing water policies at the national level and promoting green investments in several sectors by means of a guide for investors. The guide was developed as a subregional knowledge center to help in identifying and preparing bankable projects (World Bank 2020).

4.1.4 Case Study: Climate Finance Coordination via Institutionalization

Some Central and West Asian countries have shown progress in climate finance coordination for improved MRV. For instance, the Kyrgyz Republic has started institutionalizing climate finance and establishing more reliable national systems for monitoring and evaluating the implementation effectiveness of adaptation and mitigation measures, as well as their financing.

The country received $283 million in climate finance in 2018–2019, mainly for mitigation, particularly in the energy sector. In its updated NDC, the cost of implementing mitigation and adaptation actions is estimated at $10 billion; 37% of this amount will come from the country's own resources (funding by the private sector and donors, and from the national budget) and 63% will take the form of investments through international financial assistance.[6]

The promotion of low-carbon technology is a major priority for the country's renewable energy investments, which are focused on hydropower and energy efficiency. Investments will have to be made in new technologies; subsidies or incentives must therefore be introduced to make projects more bankable and financially attractive.

With respect to adaptation measures, the Kyrgyz Republic is highly vulnerable to climate impact, because of its geographic location. More adaptation finance is needed for disaster risk reduction and climate-smart development, especially in the agriculture and water sectors. Efficient water management plays a key role in the country's agricultural productivity (most of the population lives in the rural areas and works in agriculture) and energy production sourced from hydropower. More finance, as well as better adaptation measures, is needed for long-term sustainable growth through domestic job creation in renewable energy sectors and increased energy, water, and food/crop security.

Conveying the urgent need to mitigate emissions and to adapt to climate change, its country's policy frameworks indicate the effort to mobilize and diversify its sources of financing to support climate-related activities, by

- setting a more ambitious updated NDC target that promotes cleaner energy and energy efficiency as key sectors in achieving climate goals, as well as adopting a low-carbon development strategy and a national adaptation plan; and

- assigning a designated climate finance entity, the Climate Finance Centre (CFC) (Box 3), to assist in streamlining the development of climate investment programs and projects, promoting stakeholder engagement, and supporting the design, implementation, and monitoring of climate investments. The CFC was established to coordinate the country's climate-related activities across NDC sectors.

Like other countries in the subregion, the Kyrgyz Republic relies on international finance in the form of concessional project-level debt and grants. In the past decade, it received about $150 million in in ternational climate funds, sourced from climate funds, combined with cofinancing. Given its more ambitious NDC, its current state of international finance would not have been enough. Therefore, establishing the CFC was also expected to improve the MRV mechanism to better convey the reliability of climate finance data and the effectiveness of mitigation and adaptation measures, in order to attract more finance from the private sector and international sources.

---

[6]   Based on the updated Nationally Determined Contribution of the Kyrgyz Republic (2021).

**Box 3: Climate Finance Centre as Climate Finance
Coordinator Responsible for MRV Mechanism in the Kyrgyz Republic**

Most of the Kyrgyz Republic's climate financing comes from international sources, but the country has established policy frameworks to promote the financing of climate activities from diverse sources. In 2015, it started developing a strategic climate investment planning framework, the Climate Investment Programme. It also established its Climate Finance Coordination Mechanism, including a Climate Finance Secretariat, the Climate Finance Centre (CFC), to mainstream climate change considerations into sustainable development planning. The CFC coordinates climate investments and development funds in key economic sectors by serving as a bridge between the country and its major donors, MDBs, and development partners in mobilizing climate finance.

The CFC is responsible for developing and implementing a monitoring and evaluation framework. It has developed a robust MRV system to track its progress on NDC targets and finance flows, to undertake assessments of the implementation results, and to monitor and evaluate the achievement of climate targets and investment. The MRV system helped to improve climate finance mobilization, as evidenced by the increased financing received by several targeted NDC sectors and climate-related projects cofinanced from various sources—domestic, private, and international. According to the MRV system, the private sector contributed Som4.8 billion ($58.0 million), while international financing contributed Som1.2 billion ($14.5 million), targeted at biodiversity and climate adaptation projects in 2011–2016 (BIOFIN 2019).

4.2 East Asia

The East Asian countries covered in this report are rhe People's Republic of China (PRC) and Mongolia.

The subregion had a population of 1.4 billion in 2018–2019, or almost 21.5% of the total population worldwide (United Nations Department of Economic and Social Affairs, Population Division, 2022).[7]

East Asia faces significant threats from rising sea levels, extreme weather events, glacier melting, and other climate change impact. It remains one of the world's largest emitters of carbon dioxide from the burning of fossil fuels for energy and cement production. The PRC alone was responsible for almost one-third of all global carbon emissions in 2019, but it committed itself recently to achieving carbon neutrality by 2060 (Jang 2021).

4.2.1 Background of the Subregion

The subregion is characterized by a distinct continental monsoon climate and complex climate types, as it covers a large land mass with a complex topography and changes in elevation. Global warming has a direct impact on the coastal areas: it accelerates the glacier melting and the rise in sea levels. Rapid urbanization and economic growth intensify the threat posed by rising sea levels. Because of the high concentration of buildings, massive infrastructure development, and overextraction of groundwater, the land has less load-carrying capacity and is sinking at a faster rate.

Geographic location, extreme weather, and fragile ecosystems, coupled with prominent pastoral livestock and rain-fed agriculture sectors, make the PRC and Mongolian economies, as well as livelihoods and traditional cultures in these countries, highly vulnerable to climate change risk. Several extreme weather events and climate disasters have hit the subregion. In July 2021, an unpr ecedented severe rainstorm in Zhengzhou, the capital of

---

[7]   Total population of the two developing countries in East Asia, the PRC and Mongolia

Henan province in the PRC, damaged hectares of cropland and crop production, resulting in direct economic losses of around CNY53.2 billion ($8 billion) (Tao and Han 2022). Climate-induced disasters, such as droughts, storms, and flooding, caused accumulated agricultural yield losses of about $153 billion in 2008–2018, equivalent to 55% of global agricultural losses (FAO 2021). Mongolia is also vulnerable to climate change. Climate-related disaster impact, such as degradation of pastoral land and biodiversity, and increased risk of dzud (severe winter storms), has been extreme, resulting in the loss of millions of livestock.

Moreover, from their start in traditional agriculture and livestock farming, the PRC and Mongolia have transformed into carbon-intensive and extractive industry–based economies (ERI 2020; Global Economy 2020). The economy of the PRC is now influenced by the construction sector, which contributed to an overall increase of 3.9% in industrial emissions in 2020, largely as a result of steel and cement production. Mongolia's economy, on the other hand, has not only been concentrated in the extractive industries because of the country's abundant mineral deposits, such as copper and coal, but has also experienced an increasing contribution from the service sector, which has accounted for 50% of GDP in recent years.

The PRC's GHG emissions increased by 2.6% in 2019 despite a drop in the share of coal in the country's energy mix, because of higher energy consumption and greater use of oil and gas. The PRC's National Bureau of Statistics recorded the 1.5% decline in the share of coal in primary energy demand, to 57.7% in 2019 from the previous year's level. The amount of coal used in total energy consumption, however, grew by 3.3%, to 4.86 billion tons of coal equivalent. A hike in oil and gas consumption accounted for about 60% of the increase in energy emissions in 2019. The share of natural gas in the PRC's total energy mix increased to over 8% in 2019 from 4% in 2010. Compared with the PRC, Mongolia has higher carbon dioxide emissions per capita (Table 4), especially on account of its above-average energy intensity per capita, with abundant reserves of domestic coal supplying over 90% of primary energy demand and heat. Because of the extreme climate conditions, building heating systems contributed to 40% of the total heating demand, which is projected to increase by about 70% by 2030 compared with the 2010 level (IKI 2019).

The PRC's updated NDC set out more ambitious climate goals, including an increase in the share of nonfossil fuels in energy consumption to 25%, a 65% reduction in carbon intensity below the 2005 level, and the achievement of carbon neutrality by 2060 (Government of People's Republic of China 2021). Mongolia set a new target of reducing GHG emissions by 22.7% by 2030, compared with business as usual (BAU). Its updated NDC included sectors that were not previously considered, such as agriculture, waste, and several industrial sectors. In the energy sector, Mongolia committed itself to increasing the use of renewable energy sources and improving the efficiency of energy production (Government of Mongolia 2020). To achieve these goals, both Mongolia and the PRC will require a significant shift from their current fossil-heavy and carbon-intensive growth paths.

Table 4: Snapshot of Climate Change Priorities in East Asia, 2018–2019

Country	tCO$_2$e Per Capita in 2020	Net-Zero Target (Year)	LTS/LT Submission	NDC Priority Sectors	NDC Target	Finance Needs	Domestic Public Expenditure on Climate as a Share of National Budget
People's Republic of China (PRC)	8.2	2060	Submitted in Oct 2021. According to the submission, by 2060, the PRC will have fully established a clean, low-carbon, safe, and efficient energy system; reached energy efficiency, and improved the proportion of nonfossil fuels in energy consumption to over 80%	Energy, transport, low-carbon industry, adaptation (urban–rural development, built infrastructure, natural resource management, water), AFOLU (carbon sink)	PRC's first NDC (updated submission in 2021) Carbon neutrality by 2060; over 65% decrease in GHG emissions per unit of GDP from the 2005 level; increase in the share of nonfossil fuels in primary energy consumption to around 25%; increase of 6 billion cubic meters in the forest stock volume from the 2005 level; increase in the total installed capacity of wind and solar power to over 1.2 billion kilowatts by 2030	$1.4 trillion annual investment over the next decade to meet the climate targets and environmental protection standards established by the PRC in 2015 (Choi and Heller 2021)	7% on average for 2012–2019
Mongolia	11.9	Not yet announced	Not yet submitted	Energy, transport, AFOLU, adaptation (natural reserve management)	Mongolia's first NDC (updated submission in 2020) Unconditional: 22.7% GHG emission reduction (excluding LULUCF) from the 2010 level by 2030, or 44.9% GHG emission reduction (including LULUCF) from the 2010 level by 2030	$11.5 billion (2020–2030), consisting of mitigation finance of $6.3 billion and adaptation finance of $5.2 billion	N/A

AFOLU = agriculture, forestry, and land use; GDP = gross domestic product; GHG = greenhouse gas; LTS/LT = long-term strategy / long-term; LULUCF = land use, land-use change, and forestry; NDC = Nationally Determined Contribution; tCO$_2$e = metric tons of carbon dioxide equivalent.

Note: N/A = data not available. There is no disclosed information on domestic public expenditure on climate-related activities and projects as a share of the national budget.

Source: UNFCCC's NDC Registry.

4.2.2 Subregional Landscape and Key Trends

Climate finance in East Asia amounted to $418.1 billion in 2018–2019, or 81% of total climate finance tracked in this report. Most of it flowed to the PRC (99.7%); Mongolia received 0.3%. The majority of the climate finance went to climate mitigation projects (93%), chiefly in energy and transport, reflecting the PRC's plan to reach peak emission levels by 2030 in accordance with its pathway to carbon neutrality by 2060 (Government of People's Republic of China 2021).

Financing sources. Public sector commitments in 2018–2019 totaled $284.5 billion, or 68% of total climate finance in East Asia. National DFIs were the largest source of public finance (77%). Their contribution increased by 90% during the period, from $65.3 billion in 2018 to $123.9 billion in 2019. State-owned financial institutions, which accounted for 15% ($42.4 billion) of the subregion's public finance in the 2-year period, were the second-largest source. The government budget ($24.1 billion) and agencies ($22.3 billion) contributed 8% of public flows in the subregion. The private sector provided 32% of the subregion's climate finance ($133.6 billion) in 2018–2019. Corporations were the largest source of private finance; their total contribution of $51.5 billion (39% of private climate finance) went mostly to the energy sector. Households, representing 30.4% of private finance ($40.6 billion), were the second largest; 81% of their spending funded the acquisition of electric vehicles. The third-largest source of private financing, commercial financial institutions, accounted for 30% of private climate finance in the subregion, channeling their contribution through market-rate debt financing for renewable energy projects (71%) and low-carbon transportation (29%).

East Asian countries rely primarily on domestic financing. A total of $411 billion in clima te finance, mainly from the public sector, was raised and spent within the same country (the PRC) in 2018–2019. China Development Bank was the largest provider of concessional capital; local governments and SOEs made up the majority of its clients. The size of the PRC economy was one of the reasons behind the country's greater ability to mobilize finance. It even has more potential to scale up finance to meet the target of $1.4 trillion of climate investment annually (or $14 trillion over the next decade). Domestically, although private capital mobilization is a major goal of both the PRC and Mongolia, the private sector has played a limited role so far, as indicated in this report. On the other hand, international public investment from multilateral DFIs contributed a total of $7.3 billion over the 2-year period.

Sectors financed. Mitigation finance reached $390 billion (93% of the subregion's climate finance) in 2018–2019. Financing for mitigation efforts in the energy sector made up 53%, and low-carbon transport, 42%. Adaptation finance, sourced mainly from national DFIs, accounted for only 6% of climate finance during the period. The largest share of adaptation finance (55%) went to water and wastewater activities—disaster risk prevention and flood control measures, such as building sponge cities, dikes, and drainage systems—while cross-sectoral and other projects received 44%.[8] However, the amount of adaptation finance was most likely underestimated, considering the potential adaptation benefits of projects, such as those in the category of ecological construction and water management, as well as difficulties in tracking adaptation finance among private entities (Choi and Heller 2021). Figure 14 shows the breakdown of the use of climate finance in the subregion.

---

[8]   Most adaptation projects, given their cross-cutting nature, did not fit entirely into a single sectoral category.

Figure 14: Mitigation, Adaptation, and Dual-Benefit Finance in East Asia, 2018–2019
($ billion)

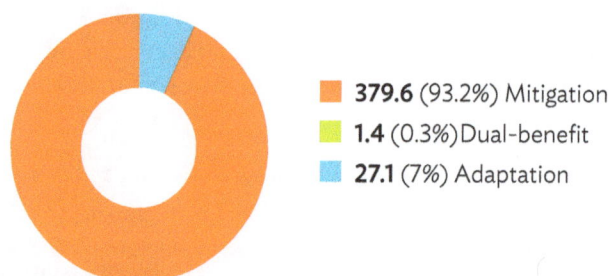

- **379.6** (93.2%) Mitigation
- **1.4** (0.3%) Dual-benefit
- **27.1** (7%) Adaptation

Source: Authors' compilation.

Financing instruments. Most of the climate finance in East Asia was raised as debt, totaling $303.1 billion (73% of the subregion's total climate finance) in 2018–2019. Of the total debt finance, $236.5 billion was provided at project-level market rates, $65.5 billion through balance-sheet financing, and $1.1 billion as low-cost project debt (Figure 15). Equity investment accounted for $100 billion, or 24% of climate finance in the 2-year period. Equity mainly supported renewable energy projects related to solar and wind onshore technologies, and electric vehicles. Grants made up the remaining 3%, or a total of $14.9 billion. Governments provided 98% of grants to finance low-carbon transportation. The PRC's decade-long central subsidy program for new energy vehicles, which was introduced initially as the Ten Cities, Thousand Vehicles project in 2009, created the world's largest electric vehicle market, accounting for half of the world's electric cars and more than 90% of electric buses and trucks (ICCT 2021).

Figure 15: Breakdown of Climate Finance Instruments in East Asia, 2018–2019
($ billion)

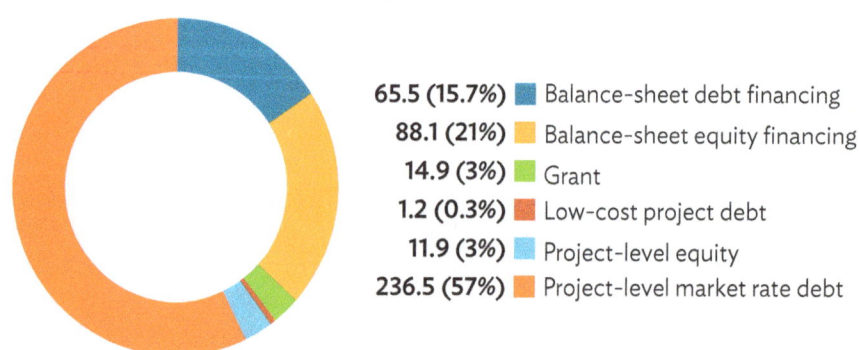

- **65.5** (15.7%) Balance-sheet debt financing
- **88.1** (21%) Balance-sheet equity financing
- **14.9** (3%) Grant
- **1.2** (0.3%) Low-cost project debt
- **11.9** (3%) Project-level equity
- **236.5** (57%) Project-level market rate debt

Source: Authors' compilation.

Impact of COVID-19 on climate finance flow. The PRC was the first country to be affected by COVID-19, and it took unprecedented lockdown measures that led to a historic decline in GDP of at least −6% in 2020. Its net GHG emissions grew around 1.7% in the wake of the pandemic, while emissions from almost all other countries declined sharply (Rhodium Group 2021). To help the country recover sustainably, ADB deployed various support programs, including (i) support for low-carbon transport and climate-resilient urban development through a bus rapid transit system, to help cities to mitigate climate-related flood risk, and risks to water security and safety; (ii) commitment of $101.4 million for river embankments to mitigate flooding, improved sewerage systems and stormwater drains, and better access to wastewater treatment for the urban population; and (iii) climate adaptation commitment of $105.5 million for climate- and disaster-resilient smart urban water infrastructure (ADB 2021b).

Mongolia, also under COVID-19 pressure, saw its GDP contract by −5.3% in 2020. To help with recovery, ADB provided support for inclusive and sustainable development through (i) climate mitigation commitment of a $100 million loan and a $3 million gr ant from the Japan Fund for Poverty Reduction (JFPR)[9] for installing 125 megawatts of advanced battery energy storage—the first such system in Mongolia and among the largest globally—to avoid 842,039 metric tons of carbon dioxide emissions annually from 2025; (ii) climate adaptation commitment of $43.6 million in support of capital city development, electricity cables, water and sewerage pipelines, and social facilities, and a $2 million JFPR grant for improving solid waste management and recycling in four secondary cities; and (iii) agriculture financing of $42 million, for the establishment of efficient and climate-resilient irrigation systems (ADB 2021a).

Gap analysis. East Asia invested a total of $418.1 billion—$171.1 billion in 2018 and $246.9 billion (or 31% more) in 2019—with a focus on mitigation efforts to reach peak emission levels by 2030. The increase in funding was attributed to strong public spending on climate projects and conducive national policies for domestic investment in renewable energy systems, as well as private spending on electric vehicles. Despite increased climate investment, however, coal still made up nearly two-thirds of the PRC's energy consumption, causing more GHG emissions in the past decade. Renewables accounted for nearly 15% of the PRC's energy mix In 2019, compared with 7% a decade earlier (Government of People's Republic of China 2021).

The PRC's updated NDC identified the need for increased adaptation efforts through the development of the National Climate Change Adaptation Strategy 2035. The strategy document, approved by the government in February 2022, strengthened the integration of adaptation actions into economic and social development, and put forward a work plan for climate change adaptation in the next 15 years (Government of the People's Republic of China 2021).

Mongolia's updated NDC determined the country's adaptation needs and priorities in broad terms, taking into consideration its specific vulnerabilities and climate risks in key socioeconomic and natural resource management sectors. Adaptation finance needs by 2030 were estimated at $5.2 billion (Government of Mongolia 2020).

Both countries expressed heightened adaptation commitment and a potentially high need for adaptation finance. However, the Global Landscape (CPI 2019a) tr acked only 6% of total climate finance destined for adaptation in the subregion. This level is hardly enough to enable the countries to face future challenges and to meet the climate ambitions set down in their NDCs.

4.2.3 Challenges and Opportunities

The PRC and Mongolia both face threats related to climate change, especially those due to the fact that large parts of their populations live near the coastline, upland steppes, semideserts, and deserts. However, not only is climate finance for adaptation scarcely available, private sector information and disclosure from the private sector is also still largely missing. Though some sectors, such as energy and transportation, are well covered, tracking adaptation finance in other sectors, such as land use and adaptation, is challenging. Data unavailability and nontransparency hinders effective analysis and the design of climate finance policy.

---

[9]   Japan Fund for Poverty Reduction (JFPR) was established in May 2000 to provide grants for projects supporting poverty reduction and related social development activities that can add value to projects financed by ADB, and was enhanced in 2021 and renamed Japan Fund for Prosperous and Resilient Asia and the Pacific, to include 4 new priority areas in addition to poverty reduction: universal health coverage, climate change and disaster risk management, quality infrastructure investment, and public finance management.

As pointed out in the Global Landscape (2019a), East Asia's heavy reliance on public finance indicates the possibility of untapped opportunities for attracting more domestic private finance, as well as foreign private capital participation. Foreign private capital accounted for less than 1% ($651 million) of inbound climate finance flows in 2018–2019. Domestic stakeholders are increasingly being encouraged to establish funds with foreign investors, and restrictions on foreign ownership are gradually being lifted (Choi and Heller 2021). Several funds have recently been established by foreign investors with participating domestic institutions. Among these are Innovator Capital's Sustainable Finance and Investment Corporation and Milltrust's Climate Impact Asia Fund. Foreign investors may also establish long-term partnerships with local businesses through joint ventures.

Given the growth potential of climate finance, thorough tracking and reporting would provide countries and prospective investors with a clearer understanding of the climate benefits of projects, and a more complete picture of climate activities and progress (e.g., the most suitable funding instruments for projects—concessional finance for adaptation vs. market-level debt for commercialized projects). Countries would then be better able to determine their climate priorities, and investors, to decide where to invest.

In East Asia, suboptimal effort to track climate finance may be due to (i) a gap in institutional capacity, making the subregion's financial systems inaccessible to private entities (but not to local governments and SOEs, which can access more concessional finance than the private sector); (ii) asymmetric information, lack of transparency, and limited detailed environmental impact reporting unsupported by a standardized methodology; (iii) undefined thresholds for meeting specific standards in green definitions and taxonomies; and (vi) lack of incentives, particularly for the private sector (e.g., subsidy, fiscal stimulus, tariff, tax), to encourage progress reporting on climate mitigation and adaptation projects.

There are opportunities for this subregion to improve the quality and transparency of climate finance data, and to streamline the definition of climate finance. Taxonomies have been developed with this in mind. For example, Mongolia's Green Taxonomy and the PRC's Green Industry Guidance Catalogue have been used in assessing the greenness of inbound financial flows to the subregion. Moves to expand the collaboration by adopting the SDG Finance Taxonomy are gaining momentum.

Taxonomies play an important role in providing direction for the adoption of disclosure and reporting standards, enabling the low-carbon transition, and adjusting common principles to suit different regional or country contexts. The first SDG finance taxonomy was developed by the PRC in 2020, and Mongolia is now developing its own version. The adoption of an SDG finance taxonomy allows the financial sector to start tracking the financial flows dedicated to the SDGs, monitor progress, and implement tailored policy incentives to support SDG financing.

4.2.4 Case Study: SDG Finance Taxonomy to reduce Information Asymmetry in Climate Finance for Private Financiers

The SDGs—global pledges that should be met by the year 2030—have driven unprecedented investment and collaboration across all sectors, including governments, the private sector, foreign investors, and international donors (e.g., grants and concessional debt from MDBs). However, there is a strong tendency for the formal financial sector to prefer large state-owned agencies with political connections, leaving smaller and private financiers behind.

The SDG Finance Taxonomy has made standardized information on SDG compliance more accessible and available, easing the way for private and international financing. The taxonomy was developed and is being used in the PRC and Mongolia as a classification system for economic activities contributing to the SDGs, along with criteria for measuring, verifying, and reporting the impact of financial flows on the attainment of the SDGs.

International climate finance in Mongolia totaled $1.1 billion in 2018–2019, mostly from three international sources—ADB, GCF, and the Import-Export Bank of Korea. In 2019, 68% of tracked finance went to biodiversity and land conservation, and 10%, to renewable energy. In 2018–2019, adaptation finance (5%) and dual-benefit finance (27%) both came entirely from international sources.

Expanding the application of a taxonomy, in 2019, Mongolia established national and sectoral coordination structures, among them, a National NDC Working Group to oversee and coordinate NDC-related processes in the country, as well as the Green Taxonomy Committee to provide clarity regardiing the activities that could qualify for green investment, including SDG-aligned, bankable economic activities (MSFA 2019).

The private sector–led Mongolian Sustainable Finance Initiative (MSFI) largely induced Mongolia's transition toward a sustainable financial system. The Mongolian Sustainable Finance Principles were launched in 2014 under the MSFI, and as a result of a joint effort exerted by the Mongolian Bankers Association, the Ministry of Environment and Tourism, and the Central Bank of Mongolia, with international support from the IFC and the Netherlands Development Finance Company (FMO). The principles were designed to help banks identify, mitigate, and manage environmental and social risks associated with their lending portfolios, push the business case for green finance, and manage their own environmental footprint.

All 15 banks in the country joined the initiative and committed themselves to abiding by its principles. The wide scope of application of the framework (all activities of financial institutions) and its support for the development of guidelines for Mongolia's four key economic sectors (mining, construction, manufacturing, and agriculture) underscored its commitment and ambition (MSFA 2019).

The Mongolia Sustainable Finance Association (MSFA) chaired the Green Taxonomy Committee, in partnership with the Central Bank of Mongolia and the Ministry of Environment and Tourism. In 2020, the Central Bank started compiling green loan statistics, to increase transparency in the private green loan market. It adopted a programmatic approach to climate finance tracking and monitoring, thus improving coordination between departments and preventing duplication and inefficiency in finance tracking and resource use.

By the end of 2020, outst anding green loans amounted to MNT371 billion ($127.3 million); 29% of this total was intended for the sustainable water and waste use sector, and 27%, for the green buildings sector (Central Bank of Mongolia 2021). Green loans currently account for only about 2% of the total loan portfolio, indicating the considerable potential for increasing green and sustainable financing.

Mongolia's green taxonomy currently covers 13 sectors and 57 subsectors (UNDP 2021b). Broader coverage is being developed with a view to attracting not only private sector contribution but also international capital flows. The taxonomy and policy incentives in support of SDG financing have been included by the Central Bank of Mongolia in the draft Monetary Policy Guidelines 2022.

Box 4: Mongolian Green Taxonomy—A "Best Practice" in Climate Finance Transparency

Several countries have developed their own green finance[a] taxonomies. Mongolia's taxonomy is among the best practices in the region.

A Green Taxonomy Committee was established in February 2019 to provide clarity regarding the activities that could be considered eligible for green investment. The taxonomy covers almost all of the country's activities and sectors, and outlines eight categories of eligible projects: renewable energy, energy efficiency, pollution prevention and control, sustainable agriculture, low-pollution energy, green buildings, sustainable water and waste use, and clean transport.

The taxonomy was developed by the Mongolian Sustainable Finance Association, and published in 2019[b] for the use of various stakeholder groups, including banks, capital market participants (e.g., bond issuers), insurance companies, and nonbank financial institutions. It is based on six principles:

- contributing to national policies and targets;
- addressing environmental challenges;
- covering high-emitting, key economic sectors;
- aligning with international standards and good practices;
- complying with environmental, social, and governance (ESG) standards; and
- engaging in continuous review and development

[a] "Green finance" refers to any financial initiative, process, product, or service that is directed at sustainable development priorities (UNEP 2016). It includes climate finance but excludes social and economic aspects. Climate finance is public finance, or financing provided by developed countries through a variety of sources, to promote multilateral efforts to combat climate change.

[b] Mongolian Green Taxonomy. https://www.ifc.org/wps/wcm/connect/0c29 6cd3-be1e-4e2f-a6cb-f507ad7bdfe9/ Mongolia+Green+Taxanomy+ENG+PDF+for+publishing.pdf?MOD=AJPERES&CVID=nikyhIh.B.

4.3 South Asia

The South Asian countries included in this report are Bangladesh, Bhutan, India, Maldives, Nepal, and Sri Lanka. The subregion covers about 5.2 million square kilometers, or 11.7% of the Asian continent, and its population of more than 1.5 billion (2021) is around 40% of Asia's, and 25% of the world's, population.

4.3.1 Background of the Subregion

The South Asia subregion is among the most vulnerable to the impact of climate change. It is the worst affected by frequent and intense extreme weather events, especially hydro-meteorological hazards like floods, droughts, hurricanes, and tornadoes, causing the greatest damage to both life and the economy (Eckstein, Künzel, and Schäfer 2021; UNESCAP 2021; IMF Climate Change Dashboard 2022). At 2°C global warming, rainfall in the region is projected to increase by 10%, compared with 7% globally, leading to more intense and frequent extreme events in the future (Schleussner et al. 2016). Drought is also projected to become more frequent because of climate change; by the middle of the 21st century, it would affect food security in the subregion, which has the largest number of food-insecure communities (IPCC 2022).

The impact of climate change has resulted in huge social, economic, and environmental loss and damage in the South Asian countries. Since 1990, more than one billion people in the subregion have been affected by floods, with fatalities numbering more than 75,000—the highest in Asia and the Pacific (UNESCAP 2021). Between 1990 and 2018, the average annual damage across the region was 0.48% of GDP; this figure was significantly higher than the global average of 0.22%, and was the highest in Asia and the Pacific. By 2030, these annual economic losses from climate impact would average $160 billion (AfDB et al. 2021). With sea levels continuing to rise, more than 40 million of the South Asian population could be climate migrants by 2050 (PIK 2013).

There is an urgent need to step up climate change action to reduce emissions and build resilience while ensuring economic growth in the subregion (World Bank 2022). All the South Asian countries have ratified the Paris Agreement and submitted their NDCs, committing themselves to reducing their GHG emissions and adapting to climate change. Table 5 outlines the NDC targets and climate change priorities.

South Asia has massive renewable energy potential, which remains untapped. The International Energy Agency (IEA), in its 1.5°C decarbonization pathway for the subregion, projects the dominance of renewables in electricity generation in South Asia within a couple of decades, reaching more than half by 2050 (Climate Analytics 2019). Decarbonization would provide environmental and economic co-benefits, such as job creation, more innovation, increased energy security, and reduced negative impact on health.

Table 5: Snapshot of Climate Change Priorities in South Asia, 2018–2019

Country	tCO_2e Per Capita in 2020	Net-Zero Target (Year)	LTS/LT Submission	NDC Priority Sectors	NDC Target	Finance Needs	Domestic Public Expenditure on Climate as a Share of National Budget
Bangladesh	0.64	–	Not yet submitted	Food security, social protection and health, disaster management, infrastructure development, research and knowledge management, mitigation and low-carbon development, and capacity building and institutional development	Bangladesh's first NDC (updated submission in 2021) Unconditional: 6.73% GHG reduction (2012–2030) Conditional: 15.12%	Adaptation needs: $230 billion (2023–2050) Conditional: $138.13 billion for mitigation (2021–2030), consisting of $131.8 billion in energy, $2.51 billion in AFOLU, and $3.76 billion in the waste sector	7.01% in 2017–2018 to 7.26% in 2021–2022

Continued on next page

Table 5 continued

Country	tCO$_2$e Per Capita in 2020	Net-Zero Target (Year)	LTS/LT Submission	NDC Priority Sectors	NDC Target	Finance Needs	Domestic Public Expenditure on Climate as a Share of National Budget
Bhutan	1.74	2030	Not yet submitted; under initiation since 2017	Forest conservation and management, sustainable agriculture, livestock, human settlements, and industries	Bhutan's second NDC, submitted in 2021 • Remain a carbon-neutral country • Formulate a National Adaptation Plan (NAP)	Conditional: $3.45 billion for mitigation, consisting of $54.5 million in forestry, $61.65 million in food security, $101.84 million in energy, and $3,233 million in low-carbon transport infrastructure development	N/A
India	1.74	2070	Not yet submitted	Energy, forestry and tree cover, adaptation through disaster management and resilient infrastructure	India's first NDC, submitted in 2016 as Intended NDC Reduce emission intensity of GDP by 33%–35% by 2030 from 2005 level	$2.5 trillion (2021–2020)	N/A
Maldives	3.63	2030	Not yet submitted	Energy, waste, adaptation (food security, infrastructure resilience, water security, coastal protection and biodiversity, and fisheries)	Maldives' first NDC (updated submission in 2020) Unconditional: 10% GHG reduction (2021–2030) Conditional: 24%	N/A	N/A
Nepal	0.6	2045	Submitted in Oct 2021 With existing measures (WEM) scenario: 30 GtCO$_2$e reduction in net CO$_2$ emissions by 2030, and 50 GtCO$_2$e by 2050	Energy, IPPU, AFOLU, and waste	Nepal's second NDC, submitted in 2020 15% of total energy demand to be met from clean energy sources	Conditional: $25 billion for mitigation (2021–2030[b])	10.34% in 2013–2014 to 30.76% in 2017–2018

Continued on next page

Table 5 continued

Country	tCO$_2$e Per Capita in 2020	Net-Zero Target (Year)	LTS/LT Submission	NDC Priority Sectors	NDC Target	Finance Needs	Domestic Public Expenditure on Climate as a Share of National Budget
Sri Lanka	1.13	2050	Not yet submitted	Energy, transport, agriculture, forestry, adaptation (water, biodiversity, coastal and marine, disaster risk management)	Sri Lanka's first NDC (updated submission in 2021) 70% renewable energy generation by 2030, 32% increase in forest cover by 2030 and 14.5% reduction in GHG emissions from power (electricity generation), transport, industry, waste, forestry, and agriculture, in 2021–2030	$3.93 billion (2021–2030), calculated on the basis of estimated loss and damage from climate change	N/A

AFOLU = agriculture, forestry, and land use; GHG = greenhouse gas; GtCO2e = gigatonnes (billion metric tons) of carbon dioxide equivalent; IPPU = industrial processes, and product use; LTS/LT = long-term strategy / long-term; NAP = National Adaptation Plan; NDC = Nationally Determined Contribution; tCO$_2$e = metric tons of carbon dioxide equivalent.

Notes:

[a] N/A= data not available. In this table's last column, the reference is to the absence of disclosed information on domestic public expenditure on climate-related activities and projects as a share of the national budget.

[b] Covers only activity-based targets, and does not include the cost of policies, measures, and actions.

Source: EU JRC 2020; UNFCCC's NDC Registry.

Per capita carbon emissions from the subregion are low, compared with the global average, but are expected to rise with population growth, and with increasing urbanization and industrialization. There is a vast disparity between the socioeconomic and emission profiles of countries in South Asia. More than 80% of emissions in the subregion are ascribed solely to India because of the country's large population and economy. Bhutan, on the other hand, is the first carbon-negative country in the world.

The subregion relies heavily on fossil fuel–based energy generation to lift the majority of its vulnerable population out of poverty. In 2021, the share of fossil fuels in India's electricity generation mix was over 60%, dominated by coal. Similarly, in Bangladesh, about 62% of energy demand is met by natural gas (Ministry of Power, Energy and Mineral Resources, Bangladesh, 2021).

Only half of the countries in the subregion have reported their financing needs for the achievement of their NDC targets, both conditional and unconditional. Access to more financial resources has been noted as a prerequisite for meeting the climate goals and targets in country NDCs. South Asian countries are already setting aside resources for climate action from their national budgets. The Government of Bangladesh, for example, spent more than 7% of its annual budget for mitigation and adaptation in 2017–2018. In Nepal, the government improved the share of climate-relevant budgeting, direct and indirect, in its total budget, from 10.34% in 2013–2014 to 30.76% in 2017–2018. Funding from domestic government made up the highest proportion (81%), followed by loans from international sources (15%), and grants (4%), highlighting the need for increased access to international climate financing (Ministry of Finance, Nepal 2018).

4.3.2 Subregional Landscape and Key Trends

Tracked climate finance for the South Asia subregion totaled $46.8 billion in 2018 and 2019. India and Bangladesh received most of the climate finance ($44.7 billion, 95% of total climate finance in the subregion during the period), from both domestic and international sources. More than half of the climate-related projects in 2018–2019, totaling $26.5 billion (56%), were funded from public sources and dedicated to climate mitigation (83%). This showed the need to scale up adaptation finance in South Asia, especially considering the subregion's climate vulnerability. Based on NDC documents of South Asian developing countries, meeting its NDC targets will require an estimated $2,727 billion in climate investments (Table 5).

Financing sources. About 45% of total climate finance in South Asia in 2018–2019 ($21.2 billion) w as raised and spent within the same country. Private investments accounted for most of these domestic financial flows (77%, or $16.4 billion), with corporations contributing the largest share (38%), followed by households (31%) and commercial financial institutions (30%). The share of domestic private finance increased by 12% during the period (from $62.5 billion in 2018 to $70.3 billion in 2019). Domestic public finance increased by 64%, from $105.3 billion in 2018 to $172.4 billion in 2019, but that was largely attributed to an increase in local government expenditure.

National governments in the subregion are progressing toward a transformation of their energy systems. Some long-term strategy (LTS) scenarios show a much faster increase in renewable energy, particularly in India, than the global rate, corresponding to the much higher increase in primary energy demand.

International flows, sourced mainly from multilateral and bilateral DFIs, accounted for 54% ($25.2 billion) of total South Asian climate finance in 2018–2019. Among the key DFIs financing projects in the region are the Japan International Cooperation Agency (JICA), the World Bank Group, ADB, the Asian Infrastructure Investment Bank (AIIB), and the KfW Group.

Sectors financed. Climate finance in 2018–2019 flo wed mostly to climate mitigation (83%), followed by adaptation (13%) and activities with dual benefits (4%). Investments in energy systems stayed almost the same; they averaged $13.1 billion per year in 2018–2019, representing 67% of the subregion's total mitigation finance and 56% of its total climate finance. Most of the renewable energy financing (78%) was targeted at solar PV and onshore wind. Key renewable energy private financiers included ReNew Power, Alfanar, Continuum Energy, L&T Infrastructure Finance Company, and Adani Green Energy.

Transport—for the most part, railway and public transport—was the second-largest recipient of climate finance (28%).

Adaptation finance went mainly to AFOLU and natural resource management (34% of the subregion's adaptation finance), and to water and wastewater management (28%). Almost all adapt ation finance was funded by the international public sector, including multilateral and bilateral DFIs and foreign governments. Its share of total climate finance stayed at 13% in 2018–2019.

Figure 16 shows the breakdown of the use of climate finance in the South Asia subregion in 2018–2019.

Figure 16: Mitigation, Adaptation, and Dual-Benefit Finance in South Asia, 2018–2019
($ billion)

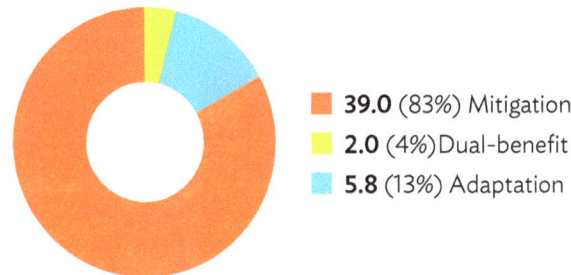

- **39.0** (83%) Mitigation
- **2.0** (4%) Dual-benefit
- **5.8** (13%) Adaptation

Source: Authors' compilation.

Financing instruments. Debt was the most widely used instrument (64%) for raising climate finance in 2018–2019 (Figure 17). But while the share of low-cost project debt decreased from 33% ($8.3 billion) in 2018 to 10% ($2.2 billion) in 2019, the share of market-rate debt at the project level grew from 26% ($6.3 billion) in 2018 to 35% ($7.6 billion) in 2019. Equity investments (32% of the subregion's climate finance), at the project level and directly on investors' balance sheets, mainly supported energy systems projects, and corporations were the primary contributors. Financing for transport projects, on the other hand, was raised through debt provided by bilateral and multilateral DFIs, at concessional and non-concessional rates.

Figure 17: Breakdown of Climate Finance Instruments in South Asia, 2018–2019
($ billion)

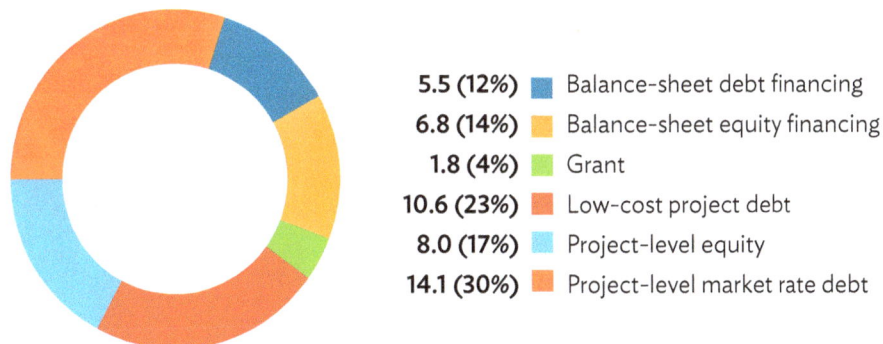

- **5.5 (12%)** Balance-sheet debt financing
- **6.8 (14%)** Balance-sheet equity financing
- **1.8 (4%)** Grant
- **10.6 (23%)** Low-cost project debt
- **8.0 (17%)** Project-level equity
- **14.1 (30%)** Project-level market rate debt

Source: Authors' compilation.

Impact of COVID-19 on climate finance flow. Worsening climate conditions already expose the subregion, in both its rural and urban areas, to a vicious cycle of risks, such as heightened energy intensity, caused by increased cooling demand as heat problems escalate. With the advent of COVID-19, the subregion and its population of up to 800 million, including some of the world's poorest and most vulnerable, have come under greater socioeconomic pressure. Recovery post-pandemic should present opportunities for the South Asian countries to adapt to and mitigate climate change by redirecting investments toward resilient infrastructure and transitioning economies around cleaner energy and sustainable land use.

Support for climate finance, mostly from the World Bank, has been identified. Climate financing in South Asia sourced from the World Bank rose from $1.4 billion in 2016–2017 to $3.7 billion in 2019–June 2021. In 2020–2021, more than $1.9 billion of this financing was for adaptation, and the rest went to climate mitigation actions (World Bank 2022).

Gap analysis. Climate investment opportunities in South Asia in 2018–2030 have been estimated at $283–$464 billion per year (IFC 2017; ADB 2017).[10] Most of the estimated investment potential lies in India, because of the scale of its economy and population, but the rest of South Asia offers substantial untapped opportunities for growth (Figure 18). In 2018–2030, sectors like renewable energy, sustainable transportation, and green buildings can unlock trillions of dollars in climate investments in all countries except Bhutan and Nepal. The Global Landscape (CPI 2019a) reported a 1,200% increase in building and infrastructure investments in South Asia, from $20.1 million in 2018 to $539 million in 2019; however, compared with the investment needs, the amount of finance flowing to the sector remains low. In the green building sector alone, investment needs across the subregion in 2018–2030 were estimated at $1.5 trillion (or $12.5 billion per year), mainly for projects in India and Bangladesh (ADB 2014). Current tracked finance in 2018–2019 therefore met only 0.5% of this sector's annual investment needs.

Climate finance in South Asia must increase at least tenfold in the next decade to meet the required investment.

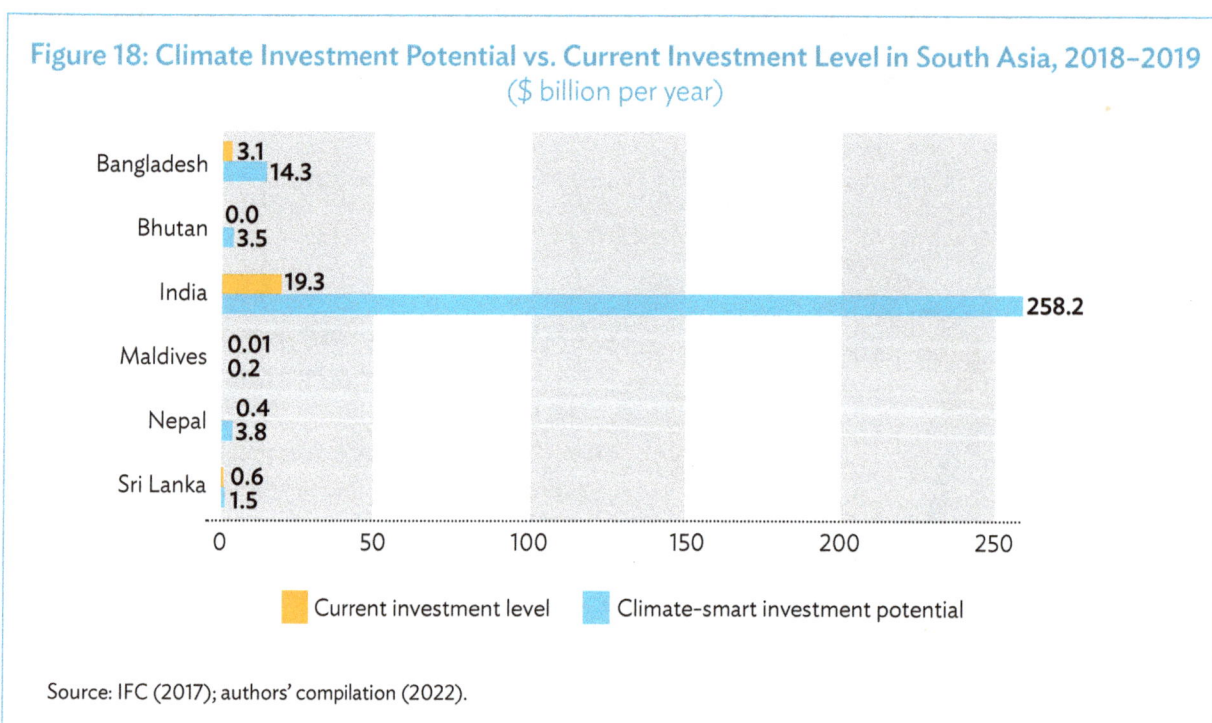

Figure 18: Climate Investment Potential vs. Current Investment Level in South Asia, 2018–2019
($ billion per year)

Bangladesh: 3.1 / 14.3
Bhutan: 0.0 / 3.5
India: 19.3 / 258.2
Maldives: 0.01 / 0.2
Nepal: 0.4 / 3.8
Sri Lanka: 0.6 / 1.5

■ Current investment level   ■ Climate-smart investment potential

Source: IFC (2017); authors' compilation (2022).

4.3.3 Challenges and Opportunities

Bangladesh and Nepal have shown substantial progress in developing climate finance tracking systems.

Three of the six South Asian countries—Bangladesh, India, and Sri Lanka—have conducted the Climate Public Expenditure and Institutional Review, a methodology for reviewing and assessing public expenditures and climate change. These countries have also adopted the Climate Fiscal Framework (CFF), which integrates climate finance into national planning and budgeting processes.

---

[10] This wide range of estimates is due to differences in scope and methodologies for estimating climate finance needs in South Asian countries.

Bangladesh and Nepal have gone a step further and localized the CFF at the subnational level to show trends in the management of climate finance and gain a better understanding of the climate vulnerability of local communities (Ministry of Finance, Bangladesh 2018). Responding to the growing demand for climate finance information from its citizens, Bangladesh has prepared a citizen's climate budget report to draw wider attention from stakeholders (Ministry of Finance, Bangladesh 2021). The results attained by these countries have been encouraging and have shown an increment in the climate-relevant portion of their national budgets. These countries are also improving the institutional capacity and resources of relevant ministries for the pilot-testing and implementation of the climate budgeting process.

However, the lack of a standardized or internationally agreed definition and taxonomy for climate finance, methodological limitations, and low institutional capacity hinder national tracking of climate finance. Climate relevance criteria followed in national budgets are often not based on scientific principles. Additionally, low-income countries do not have the institutional capacity and resources to make a comprehensive assessment of climate financing needs and flows. Tracking of private investments is also still missing or limited because of the lack of standardized and mandatory disclosure frameworks.

There is a clear opportunity for other South Asian countries to learn from the experience of other subregions in enhancing their climate finance framework. Key starting points are (i) integrating climate budgeting and tagging principles into the resource allocation process, (ii) streamlining activities related to climate finance on the basis of the agreed taxonomy, and (iii) broadening regional cooperation to attract climate-smart investment.

Currently, several departments and agencies are responsible for planning, developing, and implementing climate-related projects and activities. This dispersion of responsibility makes project monitoring and evaluation a challenging task. Taking a programmatic approach to the tracking and monitoring of climate finance could improve coordination between departments, and avoid duplication of effort and inefficiencies in resource use. Countries that already practice climate budgeting should incorporate climate change concerns and priorities into their medium-term fiscal framework and investment plans so that they can identify their mitigation and adaptation targets at an early stage of resource allocation. If climate change concerns and priorities are considered in high-level macroeconomic assumptions and the macro-fiscal baseline, climate risk management could also improve.

Countries in this subregion could likewise make use of the best-practice green taxonomy to guide further improvements in the tagging and reporting of climate-related activities, climate finance, and the impact of financial flows on the attainment of their NDCs. Moreover, in view of the rapid urbanization and economic growth in the subregion, climate finance data could induce broader cooperation among countries in directing investments toward key climate-smart solutions, such as the following:

- the green buildings sector, with India and Bangladesh leading the market;
- Bhutan's economically feasible hydropower potential of 25,000 megawatts to meet national energy needs;
- electric vehicles in India and Bhutan, given their governments' ambitious electric vehicle targets, emphasizing the need for low-carbon transport systems; and
- climate-smart agriculture in Nepal, to support the government's policy of climate-friendly agriculture and its NDC goals of increasing the use of efficient technologies and the production of local crop varieties.

4.3.4 Case Study: Taking Climate Finance Governance Forward through the Climate Fiscal Framework

South Asian countries have indicated that they will need at least $68.1 billion in climate financing to achieve their NDC targets, and that their current financing levels are clearly insufficient. A huge climate finance gap exists. Mainstreaming climate resilience into the countries' development plans should therefore be a government priority.

Bangladesh has been named among the world's fastest-growing economies (8% GDP growth in 2021), and the fastest growing in South Asia, recently surpassing India on a per capita income basis. Its carbon emissions rose 100% in the last 3 decades (1990–2020), according to country reports, but still accounted for only a small percentage of global emissions (0.35%). However, a 46% increase in these emissions by 2030 under a BAU scenario has been projected.

Various efforts have been made to mitigate the potential adverse impact of an increase in emissions. The Climate Fiscal Framework (CFF) was introduced in 2014 to provide a road map for climate finance in the country's public financial management systems—yet another significant step toward linking climate policies and strategies with the resource allocation process. Bangladesh has an annual budget for mitigation and adaptation activities, disbursed through different programs and funds. The Bangladesh Climate Change Trust Fund (BCCTF), for example, supported 789 projects with an investment of $443 million to implement strategic actions under the Bangladesh Climate Change Strategy and Action Plan 2009. CFF 2020 shows, however, that Bangladesh spends only 6%–7% of this annual budget.

Figure 19: Evolution of the Climate Financing Framework in Bangladesh

2012
Climate Public Expenditure and Institutional Review (CPEIR)
A review of expenditure on climate change activities, from domestic and international sources

2014
Climate Fiscal Framework (CFF)
Budgetary policy framework identifying existing expenditure, gaps, and opportunities, and creating an enabling framework for mobilizing climate finance

2016–2021
PMF Reform Strategy Develop strategies, policies, and institutions to mainstream SDG targets into the development framework (7th Five Year Plan, 2016–2020)

2020
Updated CFF
Broader remit, including the private sector, NGOs, and CSOs, besides highlighting relevant fiscal policies like insurance

NGO = Non-governmental organization, CSO = Civil society organization
Source: Bangladesh Climate Fiscal Framework 2020.

This report refers to two main sources of information on climate finance flows in Bangladesh—the Climate Policy Initiative's Global Landscape of Climate Finance and the government's climate budget report. These sources are not mutually exclusive and collectively exhaustive, especially because the climate budget does not provide project-level information and uses a different sectoral classification. Therefore, climate finance tracking is not possible at this stage. But the following key trends can be observed in climate finance flows in Bangladesh at the domestic and international levels:

- In 2018–2019, $3.8 billion in clima te financing came from public international sources, mainly from multilateral and bilateral DFIs (82%) and foreign governments (15%). Most of the international public financing (72%) was intended for mitigation, mainly transport (75%) and energy systems (23%). Less than 25% ($890 million) was directed toward adaptation in agriculture, water, and cross-sectoral projects. Adaptation finance tracking presents methodological challenges related to definition, attribution, and data availability.

- Regarding domestic public finance, the Bangladesh National Budget 2020–2021 contains data on the climate change–relevant allocations of 25 ministries/divisions[11] in six thematic areas, as set out in the

---

[11]   The total budget allocation of these 25 ministries/ divisions represents 56.7% of the national budget for FY 2020–2021.

Bangladesh Climate Change Strategy and Action Plan (BCCSAP) 2009: (i) food security, social protection, and health; (ii) comprehensive disaster management; (iii) infrastructure; (iv) research and knowledge management; (v) mitigation and low-carbon development; and (vi) capacity building and institutional strengthening.[12] In 2020–2021, 7.5% of the total budget allocation in Bangladesh was climate relevant. This marked a 62% increase in absolute terms over the 5-year period, from $1.6 billion in 2016–2017 to $2.9 billion in 2020–2021. A considerable portion of the allocation (41%) was for food security, social security, and health, followed by infrastructure (26%).

- The Global Landscape (CPI 2019a) noted a total of $485 million in domestic priv ate financing in 2018–2019, primarily for renewable energy projects.

Current climate finance flows are nowhere close to meeting the climate finance needs of Bangladesh. The country needs more international climate finance to achieve its climate ambition. The updated NDC submitted by Bangladesh in 2021 as sesses ambitious yet achievable GHG mitigation measures, conditional as well as unconditional. In the unconditional part of the NDC, only those mitigation measures that the country can implement by using its current local capacity and internal sources of financing are considered. Conditional emission reduction, on the other hand, will depend on international funding and technological support. GHG emissions are expected be reduced by 27.56 metric tons of carbon dioxide equivalent (tCO_2e) (6.7%) below BAU by 2030 in the unconditional scenario, and by 61.9 tCO_2e (15.1%) in the conditional scenario.

According to the NDC, Bangladesh will need around $3.2 billion per y ear to implement key mitigation measures in 2021–2030 in the unconditional scenario, and $14.4 billion per year in the conditional scenario. For the country to adapt to tropical cyclones and storm surges by 2050, it must also ha ve climate financing of around $5.5 billion per year (World Bank 2010).

The Bangladesh methodology for tracking climate finance is discussed in Box 5. Figure 19 summarizes tracked climate finance and estimated annual climate finance needs in Bangladesh.

Box 5: Climate Finance Tracking Methodology in Bangladesh

The Climate Finance Tracking Methodology in Bangladesh was developed by the government in 2018 as part of its Climate Fiscal Framework, to help in assessing the country's resource commitment to climate action. It also makes implementation more transparent, comparable, and comprehensive.

Tracking climate finance at the national level is generally far from easy. The challenges encountered include context dependency (highly related to geographic vulnerability), lack of impact metrics, and difficulties experienced in establishing causal links, disaggregating mitigation and adaptation benefits from developmental outcomes, and aggregating local benefits while measuring progress against national targets (Richmond and Hallmeyer 2019).

Several countries worldwide that track their climate finance use different frameworks and design principles in weighting climate relevance. In binary tagging, applied in some countries (e.g., Indonesia, Philippines), the entire budget for an activity is tagged as climate relevant or non–climate relevant (UNDP 2021a). In the more advanced comparative scaling approach used in other countries (e.g., Nepal, Pakistan), the relevance of an activity's stated objectives or benefits is assessed in comparison with a counterfactual scenario in order to determine weighting.

Continued on next page

---

[12]   These domestic public expenditure figures were not added to overall landscape numbers because of a lack of granular information and because of differences in sector classification.

Box 5 continued

The benefits-based approach often also considers social and economic benefits, besides the purely environmental, and for this reason typically results in a lower estimate of climate change–relevant expenditure than the objectives-based scenario. Some countries use this approach at the national level (Bangladesh, Indonesia); others have also pilot-tested it at the subnational level (Nepal, Pakistan, Philippines).

The Government of Bangladesh has adopted the objectives-based cost component approach, a cross between these two types of approach. This hybrid approach identifies and classifies climate-relevant activities, and assigns scientifically derived weights to the budget allocations made toward those activities, to estimate the percentage of climate finance. Climate finance is defined according to the additionality principle—the climate interventions made possible by climate allocations, beyond business-as-usual development financing, and the climate targets achieved as a result.

The methodology is based on a five-step process of determining the "climate sensitivity" and "climate change relevance" of an activity (see figure below). "Sensitivity" is taken to refer to a "random amount of unintended climate financing that is subsumed in Business as Usual (BAU) development financing" (UNDP, 2018). "Relevance" is the "expected amount of climate finance [compared with] BAU development financing for resilience" (UNDP, 2018).[13] The difference between these two determines the required additional financing for a specific activity.

Using this approach, the Government of Bangladesh has prepared detailed guidance on climate relevance weights for key measures and activities implemented to address the impact of climate change (UNDP 2018).

Bangladesh Climate Finance Tracking Methodology: Five-Step Approach

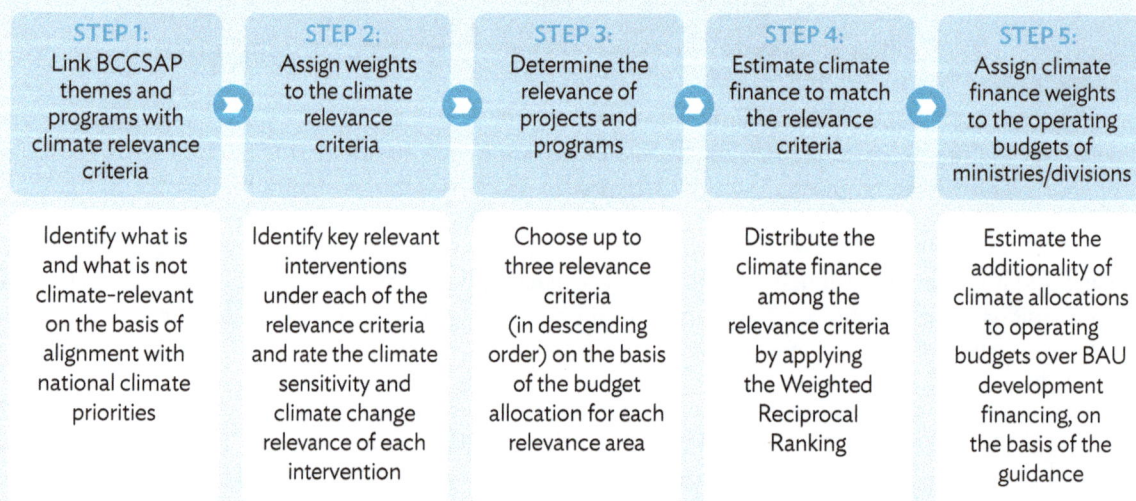

STEP 1: Link BCCSAP themes and programs with climate relevance criteria	STEP 2: Assign weights to the climate relevance criteria	STEP 3: Determine the relevance of projects and programs	STEP 4: Estimate climate finance to match the relevance criteria	STEP 5: Assign climate finance weights to the operating budgets of ministries/divisions
Identify what is and what is not climate-relevant on the basis of alignment with national climate priorities	Identify key relevant interventions under each of the relevance criteria and rate the climate sensitivity and climate change relevance of each intervention	Choose up to three relevance criteria (in descending order) on the basis of the budget allocation for each relevance area	Distribute the climate finance among the relevance criteria by applying the Weighted Reciprocal Ranking	Estimate the additionality of climate allocations to operating budgets over BAU development financing, on the basis of the guidance

BAU = Business as Usual.
Source: Ministry of Finance (MOF), Bangladesh 2021.

[13]   The fact that not all activities are equally relevant, as vulnerability varies across places and production systems, is taken into account.

**Figure 20: Tracked Climate Finance, 2018–2019,
and Estimated Annual Climate Finance Needs in Bangladesh, 2021–2030**
($ billion per year)

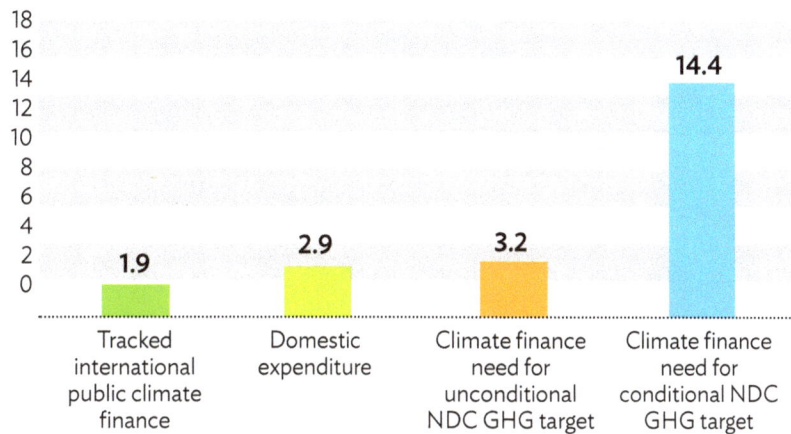

1.9	2.9	3.2	14.4
Tracked international public climate finance	Domestic expenditure	Climate finance need for unconditional NDC GHG target	Climate finance need for conditional NDC GHG target

NDC = Nationally Determined Contribution; GHG = Greenhouse gas
Note: In addition to the climate finance for Bangladesh's NDCs, the country will require on average more than $8 billion a year to implement adaptation actions under the NAP.
Source: Updated Bangladesh NDC, 2021.

4.4 Southeast Asia

Cambodia, Indonesia, Lao People's Democratic Republic (Lao PDR), the Philippines, Thailand, Timor-Leste, and Viet Nam are the Southeast Asian countries included in this report.

This subregion covers about 4.5 square kilometers—10.5% of Asia and 3% of the earth's total land area—and has a total population of 576 million, about 8% of the world's population.

4.4.1 Background of the Subregion

The Southeast Asia subregion is among the world's most vulnerable to climate change. Already, it is experiencing severe climate impact related to the current warming level of around 1°C above preindustrial levels. In the Global Climate Risk Index, the Philippines and Thailand rank among the top-10 countries most affected by extreme weather events in 2000–2019 (Eckstein, Künzel, and Schäfer 2021).

Rapid economic growth is accelerating infrastructure development in Southeast Asia. In recent years, new infrastructure construction has led to the conversion of forest, agricultural, and other land into residential, commercial, and industrial areas; altered waterways; and contributed to coastal erosion. Moreover, the population boom and urbanization are stepping up demand for energy. As more households use appliances and air conditioners, and consumption of goods and services continues to rise, electricity demand in the subregion has been escalating and is now one of the fastest growing in the world.

Over the past 20 years, there has been significant production and consumption of fossil fuels in the subregion, particularly coal, to meet demand, which is growing by more than 6% per year on average. Meeting the countries' SDGs and ambitious NDC targets has become a key challenge. Moreover, with the recent announcement of NZE targets by these countries, higher priority has been accorded to climate change mitigation and adaptation.

Table 6 summarizes the climate change priorities of the Southeast Asian countries.

Table 6: Snapshot of Climate Change Priorities in Southeast Asia, 2018–2019

Country	tCO$_2$e Per Capita in 2020	Net-Zero Target (Year)	LTS/LT Submission	NDC Priority Sectors	NDC Target	Finance Needs	Domestic Public Expenditure on Climate as a Share of National Budget
Cambodia	0.9	2050	Submitted in Dec 2020. Carbon neutrality, with AFOLU sector providing a total carbon sink of 50 tCO$_2$e	AFOLU, energy, adaptation (water resources, coastal protection, climate-resilient infrastructure)	Cambodia's first NDC (updated submission in 2021) GHG emission reduction of 64.6 million tCO$_2$e/year, or a 41.7 % reduction compared with BAU, by 2030	Conditional: Mitigation of $5.8 billion (2021–2030) Adaptation: $2 billion (2021–2030), mainly for infrastructure, water, and agriculture	Average of 4.4% of total national budget, 2017–2019
Indonesia	2.1	2060	Submitted in July 2021. Through LCCP, to reach peak GHG emissions by 2030, with net sink in forestry and land use, and toward net zero by 2060	AFOLU, energy, transport, adaptation (coastal protection, climate-resilient infrastructure, low-carbon technology)	Indonesia's first NDC (updated submission in 2021) Unconditional: 29% GHG emission reduction by 2030 Conditional: 41% GHG emission reduction by 2030	Conditional: mitigation of $23.9 billion (2021–2030), mainly for energy sector	Average of 4.3% of total national budget for 2018–2020 (or $822.3 million)
Lao People's Democratic Republic (Lao PDR)	5.8	2050	Not yet submitted	AFOLU, energy, transport, adaptation (water and waste management)	Lao PDR's first NDC (updated submission in 2021) Unconditional: 40% GHG emission reduction by 2030 Conditional: 50% GHG emission reduction by 2030	Conditional: mitigation of $4,762 million (2021–2030), mainly for increase in forest cover and renewable energy	N/A
Philippines	1.98	2050	Not yet submitted	Energy, AFOLU, adaptation (water, natural resource management, climate-smart industries, marine and coastal ecosystem)	Philippines' first NDC, submitted in 2020 GHG emission reduction and avoidance of 75% (2.71% unconditional and 72.29% conditional) in 2020–2030	$908.3 million (2021–2030), calculated on the basis of estimated loss and damage from climate change	Average of 4.0% of total national budget for 2017–2019

Continued on next page

Table 6 continued

Country	tCO$_2$e Per Capita in 2020	Net-Zero Target (Year)	LTS/LT Submission	NDC Priority Sectors	NDC Target	Finance Needs	Domestic Public Expenditure on Climate as a Share of National Budget
Thailand	3.6	2065	Submitted an updated LTS in Nov 2022	Agriculture, energy, transport, adaptation (water, natural resource management)	Thailand's First NDC (updated submission in 2020) 20% GHG reduction by 2030, compared with 2005 BAU level	N/A	Average of 0.4% of total national budget for 2017–2019
Timor-Leste	0.7	2050	Not yet submitted	Energy, transport, AFOLU	Timor-Leste's first NDC submitted in 2016 as intended NDC Not specified in NDC (note: Timor-Leste's emission level is less than 0.003% of global emissions)	N/A	N/A
Viet Nam	3.2	2050	Not yet submitted	Energy, AFOLU, IPPU, waste	Viet Nam's first NDC (updated submission in 2020) Unconditional: 9% GHG emission reduction by 2030, equivalent to 83.9 tCO$_2$e Conditional: 27% GHG emission reduction by 2030, equivalent to 250.8 tCO$_2$e	Unconditional by 2030: $24.7 billion	11% in 2018–2019

AFOLU = agriculture, forestry, and land use; GHG = greenhouse gas; IPPU = industrial processes and product use; LTS/LT = long-term strategy/long-term; NAP = National Adaptation Plan; NDC = Nationally Determined Contribution; tCO$_2$e = metric tons of carbon dioxide equivalent.

Note: N/A = data not available. In this table's last column, the reference is to the absence of disclosed information on domestic public expenditure on climate-related activities and projects as a share of the national budget.

Source: UNFCCC's NDC Registry.

4.4.2 Subregional Landscape and Key Trends

Climate finance in Southeast Asia totaled $27.8 billion in 2018–2019, or 5% of total climate finance tracked in Asia and the Pacific. Of the seven countries in the subregion, the Philippines, Viet Nam, and Indonesia—the three most populous—received the bulk of the climate finance (30%, 30%, and 23% of total climate finance in the subregion, respectively). Most of the climate finance was publicly sourced, mainly through national, multilateral, and bilateral DFIs. ADB, the biggest contributor, provided about one-third of total tracked multilateral finance in Southeast Asia, while the Japanese government was the top bilateral donor, providing more than half of total tracked bilateral finance.

Although the subregion is often referred to as one of the most vulnerable to climate change, climate adaptation assistance remained limited, at 12% of the subregion's total climate finance in 2018–2019, as noted in the Global Landscape (CPI 2019a).

Financing sources. Public finance ($18.1 billion) represented 65% of the subregion's total climate finance in 2018–2019. Multilateral DFIs were the biggest contributor, providing $6.1 billion (32% of the subregion's climate finance), followed by government budget allocations (28%, or $5.3 billion) and bilateral DFIs (24%, or $4.4 billion). Multilateral DFIs mainly supported energy projects, indicating the alignment of their funding strategy with the Paris Agreement goal of assisting developing countries in making the energy transition and building more resilient economies. The NDC documents of the Southeast Asian countries emphasize the urgency of shifting from fossil fuel–based to cleaner energy generation, and increasing the share of renewable sources in the energy mix, by 2030. Government budget allocations were provided primarily for railway and urban public transportation.

Private finance made up the remaining 35% of the subregion's climate finance in 2018–2019 ($10.1 billion), sourced in most cases from corporations ($6.5 billion, or 64% or total private finance) and commercial financial institutions ($3.2 billion, or 31%). Given the subregion's investment attractiveness, more mature technology, and bankable projects available at scale, private finance was largely directed toward renewable energy projects.

Domestic finance composed 39% ($11.3 billion) of the subregion's climate finance in 2018–2019. The highest contribution came from domestic corporations, but only half of the amount was recorded in the national budget, indicating the low availability of climate finance data and a lack of methodology for tagging and tracking climate-related activities. International finance, for its part, made up 61% ($16.5 billion of Southeast Asia's climate finance total), mostly because of increased public sector investments from international DFIs and foreign governments.

Sectors financed. Mitigation finance dominated climate finance, reaching a total of $23.4 billion (84%) in 2018–2019 (Figure 21); 50% of this total ($12.5 billion) was for renewable energy, and 42% ($10.0 billion), for transport. Agriculture, forestry, and fisheries received $467 million in mitigation finance (2%), largely from DFIs and multilateral climate funds such as REDD+, and the water and wastewater sector and the building and infrastructure sector obtained 4%.

Countries in the subregion have ambitious mitigation targets, particularly in energy, where a sizable financing gap is likely. The accelerated energy transition in Southeast Asia aligns with the findings of the IPCC special report on the impact of global warming of 1.5°C (IPCC 2022). According to the report, to reach net-zero emissions by midcentury and keep global warming from exceeding 1.5°C, as called for in the Paris Agreement, countries must rapidly decarbonize their energy systems.

Adaptation finance ($3.4 billion) accounted for only 12% of climate finance in Southeast Asia in 2018–2019, despite the subregion's high vulnerability to climate change. Mainly internationally sourced, adaptation finance went to priority adaptation sectors, including land-use change and forestry, natural resource management, and water and wastewater management. Institutional strengthening, capacity building, and other actions intended to facilitate policy-making also received adaptation finance.

The rest of the climate finance in Southeast Asia in 2018–2019 ($1.1 billion, or 4% of the subregion's total) supported cross-sectoral projects with dual benefits.

Figure 21: Mitigation, Adaptation, and Dual-Benefit Finance in Southeast Asia, 2018–2019
($ billion)

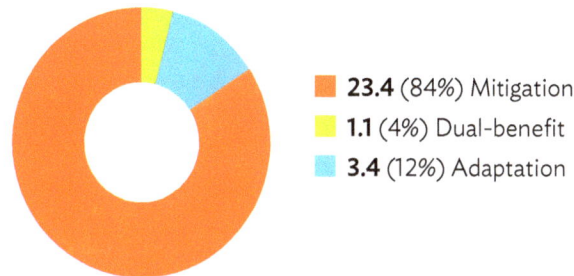

- **23.4** (84%) Mitigation
- **1.1** (4%) Dual-benefit
- **3.4** (12%) Adaptation

Source: Authors' compilation.

Financing instruments. Of Southeast Asia's climate finance total in 2018–2019, 68% ($19.0 billion) took the form of debt funding, mostly at the project level. Project-level debt totaled $14.4 billion, with low-cost debt and market-rate debt in almost equal proportions. Low-cost debt was sourced primarily from bilateral DFIs ($4.3 billion, or 57% of total low-cost debt); market-rate debt, from multilateral DFIs ($5.1 billion, or 68% of total market-rate debt). Balance-sheet debt financing, mainly from corporations (50%) and c ommercial financial institutions (35%) and in tended for renewable energy projects, reached $4.6 billion in 2018–2019.

Debt instruments were growing in volume and variety (e.g., green bonds and sukuk,[14] green credit facilities, blended finance), amid the rising popularity of sustainable finance globally and in the subregion. Concerns were raised over the prospect of a heavy debt load, which could erode the financial capacity of recipient countries.

Equity investments accounted for 27% of the total climate finance in the subregion in 2018–2019. These flowed almost exclusively to energy investments, such as renewable energy generation, transmission, and distribution, and energy efficiency. Corporations, for the most part, supplied capital through direct placement (balance-sheet equity finance), while governments provided project-level equity support.

Grants accounted for only 5% ($1.3 billion) of the subregion's total climate finance. Cross-sectoral investments and AFOLU were the main recipients.

Figure 22 breaks down climate finance in the subregion in 2018–2019 according to the types of financing instruments used.

---

[14] Green sukuk are Sharia-compliant bonds issued to finance climate change mitigation and adaptation.

Figure 22: Breakdown of Climate Finance Instruments in Southeast Asia, 2018–2019
($ billion)

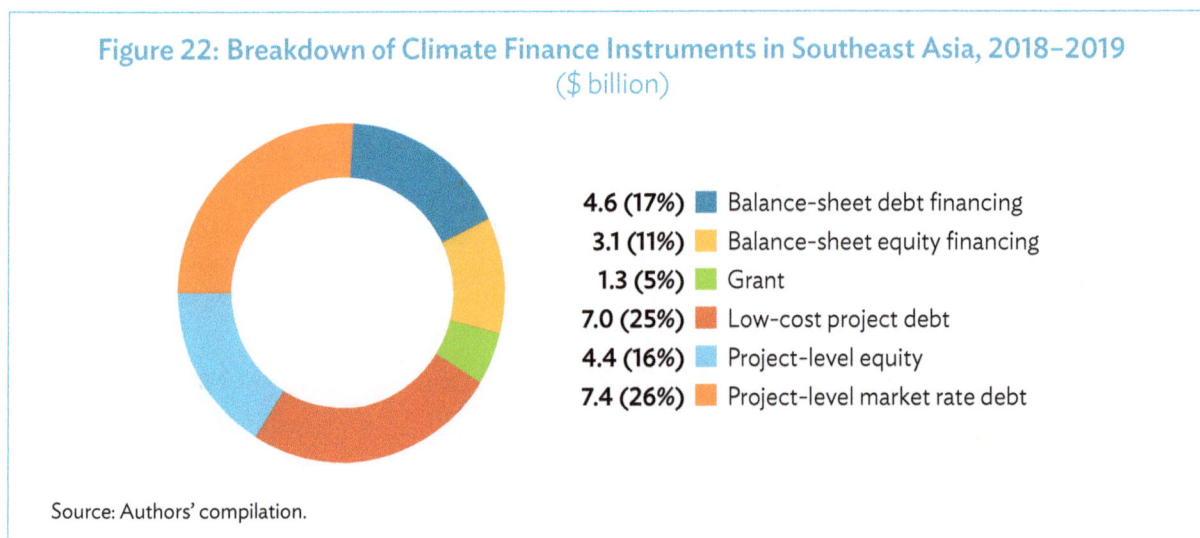

4.6 (17%) ■ Balance-sheet debt financing
3.1 (11%) ■ Balance-sheet equity financing
1.3 (5%) ■ Grant
7.0 (25%) ■ Low-cost project debt
4.4 (16%) ■ Project-level equity
7.4 (26%) ■ Project-level market rate debt

Source: Authors' compilation.

Impact of COVID-19 on climate finance flow. As in other subregions, economic activity in Southeast Asia has experienced the adverse impact of COVID-19, as evidenced by the contraction in GDP growth to –3.2% in 2020. Key sectors and business operations, particularly the travel, tourism, retail, and services sectors, have been affected, and supply chain disruptions have occurred as a result. In addition, there has been a decline in consumer purchasing power and investor confidence in the subregion due to political uncertainly.

Climate finance mobilization has slowed during the pandemic. Though the slowdown is not significant, the Global Landscape (CPI 2019a) recorded a decrease in tracked finance from $14.0 billion in 2018 to $13.8 billion in 2019. Local governments, the main source of domestic climate finance, have rolled out various measures to counter the impact of the pandemic, including wage subsidies, fiscal stimulus packages, cash assistance, and interest rate subsidies. Budgets have had to be reallocated, to fund the recovery package, resulting in fiscal pressure. With the drop in international climate finance mobilization in 2018–2019, the climate finance gap has widened further.

During the global economic contraction due to COVID-19, some Southeast Asian countries have raised their climate ambitions and defined higher goals in the updated NDCs they submitted to the UNFCCC in 2020 or 2021. Seven countries have set tougher emission reduction targets, contingent on the receipt of funding assistance from advanced economies for their long-term climate goals (Martinus and Jiahui 2022).

In 2021, in ternational funders collectively pledged $665 million in funding as sistance for the Association of Southeast Asian Nations (ASEAN) Catalytic Green Finance Facility (ACGF), a platform managed by ADB that is designed to mobilize an additional $7 billion for low-carbon and climate-resilient infrastructure projects in Southeast Asia and to accelerate the subregion's recovery (ADB 2021d). The financing and technical assistance provided is intended to reduce investment risks and catalyze public and private financing for green infrastructure projects, supporting the countries' efforts to achieve their climate goals and to strengthen green capital markets (by expanding the issuance of green bonds).

Gap analysis. Adaptation finance in the subregion has been challenging because of its fragmented nature and difficulties in obtaining precise and granular finance-related data. This was evidenced by the data disparity between the Global Landscape (CPI 2019a) and national communications submitted to the UNFCCC. The fourth, fifth, and sixth national communications reported a total of only $3.9 billion in Southeast Asia climate finance, including only $0.6 billion for adaptation (or 15% of the subregion's climate finance total reported to the UNFCCC). These figures were lower than those tracked in the CPI report. The Global Landscape identified a total climate finance of $27.8 billion and adaptation finance of $3.4 billion in the subregion (excluding Brunei, Malaysia, and Singapore).

The proportion allocated to adaptation in the subregion was high for Indonesia (36%), the Philippines (17%), Cambodia (14%), and Viet Nam (9%). Most adaptation funding is sourced from international DFIs, but there is vast room for improvement in national government funding. The existing national budget can be optimized to align more closely with adaptation needs.

The need for adaptation financing in the subregion has been rising and is expected to increase even faster, for the following reasons:

- High levels of economic activity on the Southeast Asian coast. The subregion has one of the longest coastlines in the world, at 234,000 kilometers. Major coastal cities and key ports account for over 60% of GDP in some countries. Around 77% of the population of the subregion lives in coastal areas (PEMSEA 2015), and around 39.4% (229 million) live in vulnerable coastal areas below the high-tide line (Kulp and Strauss 2019). Indonesia has the greatest number of people living below the high-tide line (72 million), followed by Viet Nam (60 million), the Philippines (36 million), Thailand (22 million), Malaysia (12 million), Cambodia (7.1 million), Singapore (1.9 million), and Brunei (0.22 million) (Kulp and Strauss 2019).

- High pressure from increased frequency of disasters in the subregion. The ASEAN Coordinating Centre for Humanitarian Assistance on disaster management (AHA Centre) reported a total of 35 disasters in Southeast Asia in 2022, during Week 23 (6–12 June) and Week 24 (13–19 June). Social as well as economic losses resulting from the floods, landslides, storms, earthquakes, and wind-related disasters were heaviest in Indonesia, the Philippines, and Thailand. For the past 20-year period, Thailand reported the highest loss from extreme weather–related events (0.87% of GDP), followed by the Philippines (0.57%) and Viet Nam (0.47%) (Eckstein, Künzel, Schafer, and Winges 2020). More recently, 10.6 million people in the Philippines were affected (EM-DAT 2022), and an estimated economic cost of $22 million in rebuilding aid over 24 months was incurred, when Typhoon Rai hit the country in December 2021 (IFRC 2022).

4.4.3 Challenges and Opportunities

Southeast Asia is also faced with the issue of **uneven adaptation–mitigation funding, limiting the countries' capacity to reverse the effects of climate change and to make their vulnerable populations more climate resilient.** While the magnitude of adaptation finance has grown over the years, the speed of funding has yet to catch up with the ever-rising adaptation finance needs of the subregion. Financiers still perceive climate adaptation projects as risky because (i) planning and implementation take longer, and are more exposed to high political risk as a result; and (ii) projects are smaller in scale, and therefore cost more per dollar raised.

Private sector contribution remains crucial but limited, considering its untapped sources of financing and expertise. Financiers still tend to prefer mitigation to adaptation actions because (i) the return on investment can be capitalized more quickly, (ii) the climate-related impact is apparent (e.g., GHG reduction, with the possibility of carbon offsetting and trading), and (iii) the carbon reduction market and technology have been more favorable in the last decade, e.g., less costly solar and wind energy generation.

Without private sector investment, meeting resilient infrastructure financing needs would be a challenge. In their NDC documents, the Southeast Asian countries identify climate finance needs of up to $68.1 billion in total by 2030. Rapid economic growth is pushing these countries to invest more in adaptation, particularly in climate-smart infrastructure. Indonesia, for instance, just announced its need for $429.7 billion in infrastructure investments in 2020–2024 (20% more than the $359.2 billion required in 2015–2019). Its fiscal capacity is expected to cover only 30% of this requirement; the rest will most likely come from nongovernment funding (Ministry of National Development Planning, Indonesia, 2020). Given the large amounts of financing needed to meet the countries' climate change commitments and infrastructure investments, private sector engagement has a vital role not only in closing the gap in financing and implementation but, more importantly, in ensuring the long-term financial sustainability of these investments.

The private sector is crucial to the development and implementation of climate projects because of its sector-specific expertise, technology, efficiency, financing, and entrepreneurship (Ministry of Finance, Indonesia, 2021). Investors and businesses are trying to manage their exposure and vulnerability to climate risks accross their value chain, business process, and investment decisions. Their involvement will help in tapping new adaptation-related business opportunities, such as in developing markets for new goods and services that support the strengthening of climate resilience, and designing financing mechanisms and business models for the implementation of adaptation priorities.

Adaptation programs are now largely treated as add-ons to development programs, and not as an integral part of the programs. Southeast Asian countries should regard adaptation as an extension of sustainable development practices intended to build resilience and minimize the costs of emissions that have been locked into the climate system. Mainstreaming adaptation into development policy could serve to redirect the finance to areas or sectors with the most impact. National policy practices, such as fiscal discipline, climate budget tagging, and strategic public spending to attract private sector contribution, would improve the efficiency and effectiveness of available financing.

The window of opportunity for addressing the climate crisis is rapidly shrinking, and governments must consider further efforts to rebalance the risks to shareholders with the urgency of responding to the climate adaptation needs of the most vulnerable countries.

Lack of institutional readiness has constrained the countries' access to various climate finance sources. Indonesia, in 2019, formed the Environmental Fund Management Agency (BPDLH) to channel and distribute environmental and climate funds, but still has limited capacity to translate needs into high-quality projects and to meet the fund access criteria and requirements of resource providers, such as the GCF. The BPDLH is not yet an accredited entity of the GCF.

In the Philippines, the Climate Change Commission (CCC) has been working with various government agencies to increase capacity and eligibility for international funding through interagency coordination. Lessons have been shared among the focal points to enable the development of screening and evaluation tools for assessing the quality of project proposals, paving the way for more streamlined climate finance tracking and reporting across the subregion, through intra-ASEAN cooperation. For instance, the ASEAN Comprehensive Recovery Framework was established in anticipation of the post-COVID recovery, to integrate the member countries' strategies for a green recovery and just transition, involving specific programs in support of clean energy, climate-smart agriculture, and sustainable forest management. The streamlined framework will require enhanced reporting to secure and mobilize public and private funding.

Determining the accuracy of climate change finance data has been a challenge for years, and the difficulty has been even more pronounced when it comes to adaptation finance data. The Global Landscape (CPI 2019a) notes that adaptation finance data are mostly fragmented and hard to obtain because of the lack of precise and comprehensive national-to-local (project-level) finance-related data for individual countries.

Climate budget tagging (CBT) or climate change expenditure tagging (CCET), used in some countries to account for financial flows, makes public investment information more available, and therefore enables governments and their agencies to determine and prioritize adaptation initiatives with the most impact in the subregion. The use of such tools could also increase the capacity of the public–private partnership funding system. ASEAN is developing the ASEAN Climate Finance Mobilization and Access Strategy to harmonize the use of more bottom–up and peer-to-peer sharing of tools and frameworks for tracking finance flows in the subregion.

Concrete quantitative targets must be set for financial resource mobilization and support, and the scale of the climate finance needed to make a significant impact on climate change must be determined. Many countries have indicated their need for external short-term financial support for more urgent climate programs tailored to their specific circumstances, as well as for long-term financing for policy formulation and the development of resource mobilization strategies.

There is massively underused potential for subregional collaboration in climate finance under ASEAN leadership. Only a few collaborative projects have been developed so far across the member states, as reported in the Global Landscape (CPI 2019a). Such flagship projects would not only help the members reach their NDC climate ambitions, but also improve the visibility of ASEAN efforts worldwide and narrow the knowledge and institutional gaps. Collective learning would also increase the capacity of member states to develop bankable projects and access international funds. ASEAN has been working to harmonize guidelines for financing project loans, such as the ASEAN Taxonomy for Sustainable Finance and the ASEAN Green Bond Standards, to provide the subregion with a common language for communicating their climate vision to a wide range of investors so they can play more critical roles in filling the financial gaps in the future.

4.4.4 Case Study: Enhancing the Climate Finance Ecosystem and using Country Platforms to Improve Accessibility and Tracking of Finance

Recognizing that relying on national budgets alone will not be enough, governments have urgently been looking into untapped resources and new means of financing, including innovative finance mechanisms. In Southeast Asia, the countries have acknowledged the joint effort needed to create a sustainable finance ecosystem in order to channel more climate funding into suitable priority sectors. This subregion is a unique construct with its own context and needs. Member states are economically and socially diverse. An orderly transition must be made toward a low-carbon and more sustainable economy.

Indonesia, in 2014, introduced the Sustainable Finance Roadmap, a binding regulatory framework for green finance that could include compulsory environmental and social management systems and associated reporting, as part of a joint effort to reduce emissions and tackle the long-term impact of climate change. This member state, with a population of 270 million, faced the risk of a three- to fourfold increase in extreme weather events by 2050. The climate change impact could cost 2.5%–7% of Indonesia's GDP by 2100, according to ADB estimates (ADB 2021c).

Adapting to the climate impact induced by rapid population growth, on the other hand, would require $429.7 billion in infrastructure investments for 2020–2040, as estimated by the Ministry of National Development Planning. The country's infrastructure development targets for 2022 include climate-smart infrastructure, such as solar power plants, sustainable urban transport systems and irrigation networks, and clean water and sanitation access (Figure 23). Directing efforts—financial aid, policy support, and other enabling activities—toward climate adaptation was an increasingly urgent concern.

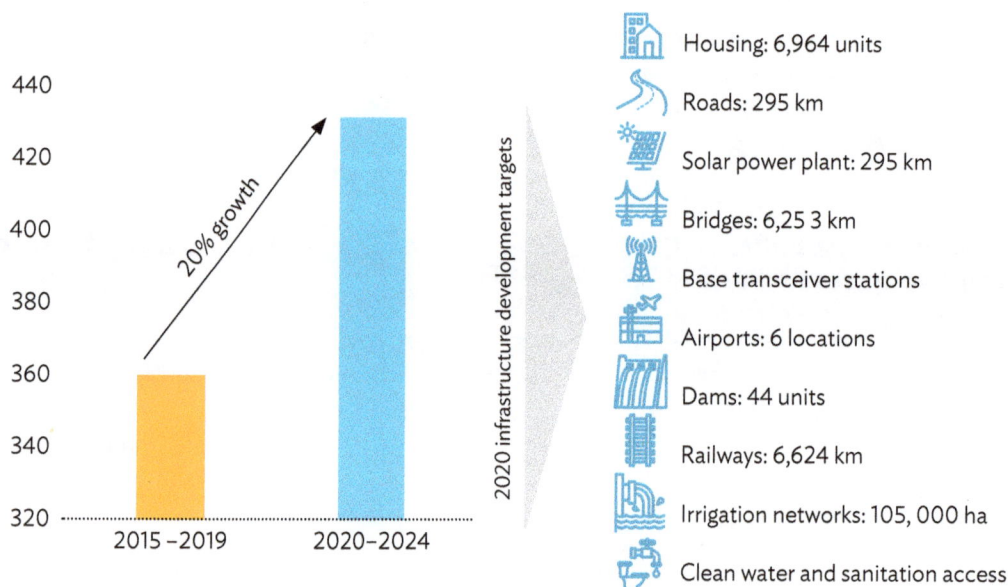

Figure 23: Infrastructure Investment Needs in Indonesia, 2020–2040
($ billion)

Housing: 6,964 units
Roads: 295 km
Solar power plant: 295 km
Bridges: 6,25 3 km
Base transceiver stations
Airports: 6 locations
Dams: 44 units
Railways: 6,624 km
Irrigation networks: 105, 000 ha
Clean water and sanitation access

Sources: Ministry of National Development Planning, Indonesia (2020); Ministry of Public Works and Public Housing, Indonesia (2020).

For climate change mitigation, Indonesia has committed itself to a 29% unconditional reduction in GHG emissions from the BAU level by 2030, or a 41% reduction with international assistance. At least $263.5 billion in climate financing in 2020–2030 would be required (Table 7). Reaching peak GHG emissions by 2030 is the intermediate goal of the country's Long-Term Strategy for Low Carbon and Low Resilience 2050, which looks forward to carbon neutrality by 2060 at the earliest. Decarbonizing the energy sector would account for 83% of the needed financing for climate mitigation. Massive investments would have to be made in renewable energy to retire fossil fuel–fired power plants and build storage, transmission and distribution, and electric vehicle infrastructure to achieve NZE in the sector. The financing needs would be higher if adaptation needs were included, but the state budget has limited fiscal capacity, particularly during COVID-19.

Table 7: Indonesia Climate Mitigation Investment Needs (Total 2020–2030),
Based on Updated NDC

Sector	Investment Amount ($ Billion)
Energy and transport	244.1
IPPU	0.06
Waste	12.6
Agriculture	0.3
FOLU	6.5
Total	263.5

FOLU = forestry and land use; IPPU = industrial processes and product use.
Source: Indonesia's updated NDC, 2021.

Furthermore, climate investments made so far in Indonesia have shown the following trends:

- The state budget contributes no more than 34% of the total needed to achieve the country's NDC 2030 target, assuming that the line ministries provide for low-carbon development in their annual budget. In 2014, Indonesia introduced the use of mitigation budget tagging (Low Emission Budget Tagging and Scoring System) in key ministries to track resources spent to meet the national emission reduction target. Two years later, the Climate Budget Tagging (CBT) mechanism started to be implemented at the national level (Box 6). CBT implementation was expanded to the subnational level in 2020. The subnational CBT has been pilot-tested in several provinces, cities, and regencies, with support for local governments in capacity building and training of staff, as well as in data monitoring and evaluation. CBT is one of the grand strategies intended to strengthen Indonesia's climate finance governance by optimizing the available fiscal capacity to finance national climate goals.

- The private sector can contribute only up to 49% of the total funding the country needs to achieve its NDC 2030 target. This could be an indication of the following: (i) limited government policy incentives for the green sectors, and (ii) deficiencies in private finance tracking due to a lack of clear and comparable data and the use of different climate finance metrics.

The remaining 17% of Indonesia's total climate finance needs should be covered by other sources, such as international funding. International funding flows to Indonesia are commonly provided by means of three funding instruments: (i) international debt, almost evenly divided between the public (60%) and private (40%) sectors; (ii) international grants, mostly (85%) to the public sector; and (iii) foreign capital flows (mainly equity), almost exclusively directed toward the private sector, in the business-to-business scheme.

The Global Landscape (CPI 2019a) supports the argument that access to, and mobilization of, international finance has been less than optimal. International public institutions and parties have pledged $700 million in funding for climate actions in Indonesia, however, by 2019, only around $301 million, less than half of the commitment had been disbursed (Climate Funds Update 2021). Several government-led fund institutions and platforms have been created to improve access to international climate funds (Table 8). These have introduced distinct strategies for eliminating investment barriers to make the climate projects more attractive.

Table 8: Public International Climate Finance Access and Mobilization in Indonesia

Platform	Area of Intervention	Funding Source	Commitment ($ billion)	Disbursement (%, est.)	Disbursement Modalities	Strategies for Eliminating Investment Barriers		
						Selection of Project Pipelines	Project Matching with Available Funding	Accountability Framework and Reporting
Indonesia Climate Change Trust Fund	Entire mitigation and adaptation sectors	$29 million has been raised from bilateral (USAID, UK–CCU, DANIDA, BMUM) and multilateral sources	29.9	100%	Grant-based funding through implementing partners (ministries, universities, and CSOs)	Eligible projects shortlisted in the call for proposals will later enter proposal development stage for detailing, before being approved by the ICCTF board		Clinic coaching and financial spot-checking
Environment Fund (BPDLH)	Entire mitigation and adaptation sectors	Funding can come from both state budget and international sources Current commitment from multilateral (FCPF, BCF, GCF) and bilateral (Norway) sources	833	N/A	Direct disbursement to beneficiaries or intermediaries (financial institutions, subnational gov'ts, CSOs)	• BPDLH or its intermediaries may provide technical assistance for the management of activities and financial reporting	• Leveraging of state budget and fines for project financing, e.g., disaster pooling fund (PFB), social forestry budget, carbon tax, e-waste fines, mangrove fund • Legal right to lend (e.g., through a revolving fund) based on donor agreement	• Requirement to list projects in the national registry system (SRN) • Requirement to submit annual activity and financial reports
SDG Indonesia One	Energy and all adaptation infrastructure projects	Private (corporations, donors/ charities, financial institutions, institutional investors) and public (multilateral/ bilateral)	3,250	20%	Disbursement modalities based on cooperation model: (i) on balance sheet (loans, grants) and (ii) off balance sheet (grants, TA)	• Project development facilities for project feasibility studies • Technical assistance for pre-FS, FS, and ESIA preparation • Capacity building for project implementers	• De-risking grant facilities to reduce project's inherent risk • Low-cost lending and equity financing	• On-balance-sheet or off-balance-sheet accounting

USAID = U.S. Agency for International Development; UK–CCU = UK Climate Change Unit; DANIDA = Danish International Development Agency; BMUM = Federal Ministry for the Environment, Nature Conservation, Building and Nuclear Safety – German Government; BCF = Biocarbon Fund; BPDLH = Indonesian Environment Fund/Badan Pengelolaan Dana Lingkungan Hidup; CSO = civil society organization; ESIA = Environmental and Social Impact Assessment; FCPF = Forest Carbon Partnership Facility; FS = feasibility study; GCF = Green Climate Fund; ICCTF = Indonesia Climate Change Trust Fund; PFB = Pooling Fund for Disasters/ Pooling Fund Bencana; SDG = Sustainable Development Goals; SRN = National Registry System/ Sistem Registri Nasional; TA = technical assistance.
Sources: Climate Funds Update (2021); ICCTF (2020); PT SMI (2020); BAPPENAS (2021).

Knowing the amounts of financial flows to developing countries, the nature of the funded activities, and the source of the funding is essential for coordinated and predictable climate finance, particularly adaptation finance. The country platforms are mandated to manage the funds and mobilize them to cover all NDC priorities, while also tracking and reporting the magnitude and performance of the funds periodically. This information helps donors, existing as well as potential, in reassessing their funding strategies for their commitments under the common but differentiated responsibility principle, to ensure that all vulnerable countries and communities receive their fair share of funding and that the most impactful sectors benefit.

Box 6: Strengthening Indonesia's Climate Finance Ecosystem through Climate Budget Tagging and Country Platforms to Improve Climate Finance Tracking

Indonesia has developed climate budget tagging (CBT) and implemented it in key ministries to track resources spent toward its national emission reduction target. CBT, integrated into the national planning and budgeting system, is a tool for identifying and tracking the amounts spent by the government on climate change mitigation and adaptation by tagging all spending that fits in with the government's climate objectives. The figure below outlines Indonesia's climate budget tagging process.

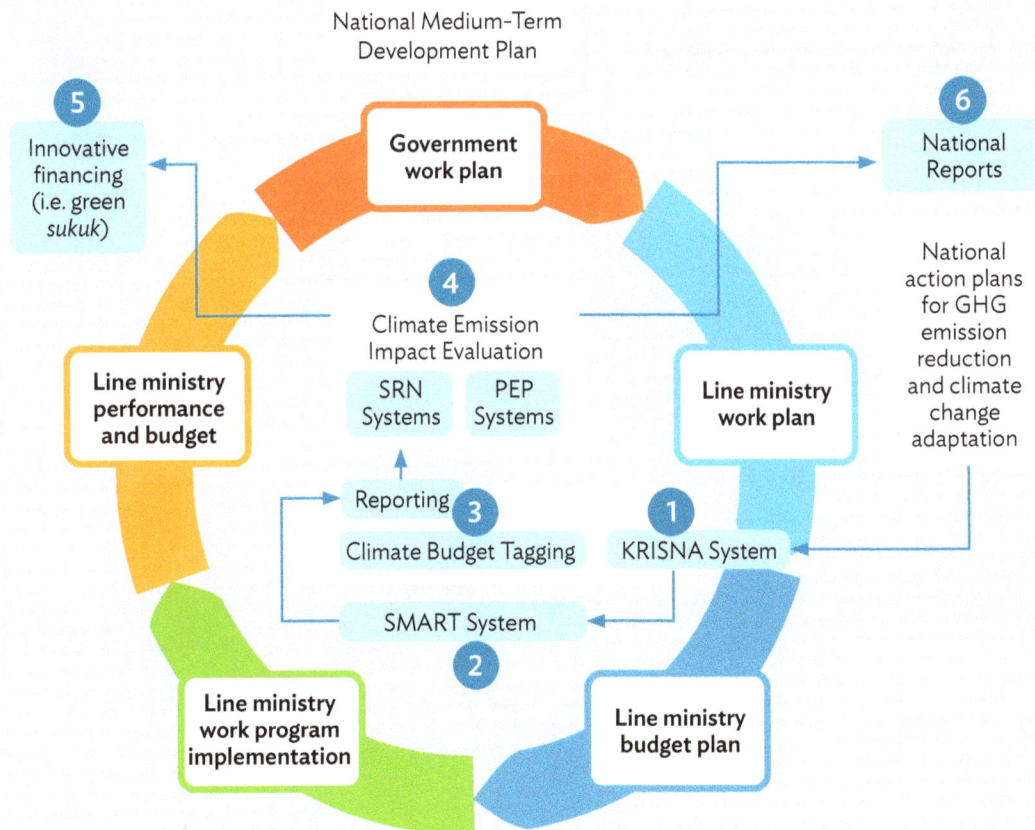

CBT provides the government with the insights needed to fund national commitments because CBT

- identifies and prioritizes climate change–related investment to support "green budgeting;"

- acknowledges the need for transparency and improved accountability in government spending; and

- mainstreams climate change actions into national development programs, thus helping policy makers to redirect and align their fiscal and expenditure policies and regulations.

Indonesia's Climate Budget Tagging Process

National Medium-Term
Development Plan

5 Innovative financing (i.e. green *sukuk*)

6 National Reports

National action plans for GHG emission reduction and climate change adaptation

Government work plan

4 Climate Emission Impact Evaluation

SRN Systems   PEP Systems

Line ministry work plan

Line ministry performance and budget

Reporting

3 Climate Budget Tagging   1 KRISNA System

SMART System

2

Line ministry work program implementation

Line ministry budget plan

Source: Fiscal Policy Agency, Ministry of Finance, Indonesia 2019.

Continued on next page

Box 6 continued

In addition, to strengthen Indonesia's climate finance ecosystem, the following country platforms, among others, were introduced to attract more international funding:

- **Indonesia Climate Change Trust Fund (ICCTF).** The ICCTF supports Indonesia's 26%/41% emission reduction target by leveraging domestic resources and international funds and channeling these into projects aligned with Indonesia's national and subnational implementation plans for climate change.

- **SDG Indonesia One.** This platform has four pillars tailored to the risk appetite of donors and investors: Development Facilities, De-risking Facilities, Financing Facilities, and Equity Funds. It aims to raise funding from investors, donors, and philanthropists to be channeled to projects in Indonesia that support the achievement of the Sustainable Development Goals.

- **Environmental Fund Management Agency** *(Badan Pengelola Dana Lingkungan Hidup, or BPDLH).* This environmental funding mechanism for channeling and distributing environmental and climate funds brings different sources of funding together to be deployed through a variety of instruments across the sectors addressed in the Nationally Determined Contribution (NDC), including forestry, energy and mineral resources, carbon trading, environmental services, industry, transport, agriculture, and marine and coastal fisheries.

By 2019, these platforms had tracked a total of $4.1 billion in international funding commitments to support Indonesia's climate program (see figure below).

International Funding Commitments Tracked by Country Platforms by 2019
($ million)

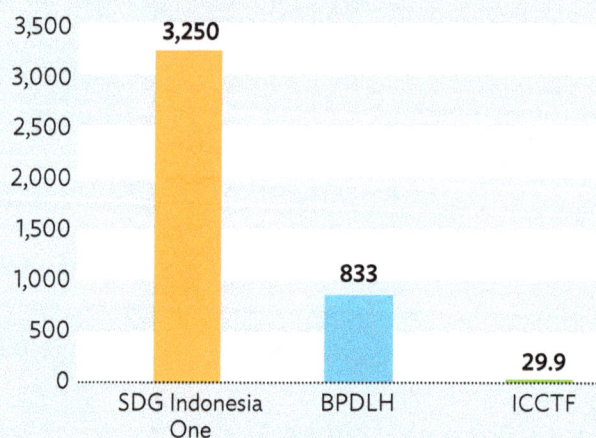

SDG = Sustainable Development Goal; BPDLH = Badan Pengelola Dana Lingkungan Hidup (The Environmental Fund Management Agency); ICCTF = Indonesia Climate Change Trust Fund.
Sources: Climate Funds Update (2021); ICCTF (2020); PT SMI (2020); BAPPENAS (2021).

4.5 Pacific

The Pacific countries covered in this report are the Cook Islands, the Federated States of Micronesia, Fiji, Kiribati, the Marshall Islands, Nauru, Niue, Palau, Papua New Guinea, Samoa, Solomon Islands, Tonga, Tuvalu, and Vanuatu.

The Pacific is the largest oceanic continent in the world, covering 15% of the global surface and having a total population of over 11.9 million. Its boundaries extend from the Arctic Ocean in the north to the Southern Ocean in the south, and it is bounded by Asia and Australia in the west and the Americas in the east. All the 14 Pacific small island developing states are parties to the UNFCCC and have ratified the Paris Agreement.

4.5.1 Background of the Subregion

The Pacific has experienced significant climate change effects, environmental damage, poverty, and other social challenges. This underlying vulnerability is due to the geographic condition of the countries, being small in size, and remote from domestic and international markets, resulting in high cost of logistics and a narrow resource base. Three Pacific countries covered in this report are listed among the top 10 most at-risk countries in the world: Vanuatu and Tonga rank first and second, and the Solomon Islands ranks fourth (Day, S. et al. 2019).

The population is concentrated in the coastal areas, making the subregion more exposed to the impact of rising sea levels, such as increased inundation and flooding, and saltwater intrusion into aquifers. These risks have forced coastal communities to relocate further inland or migrate to a different country. Fiji and Kiribati, for instance, have relocated significant portions of their population because of increasing coastal erosion and saltwater intrusion, in anticipation of the continued effects of climate change (Ministry of Economy, Fiji, 2019). The rate of sea level rise in some parts of the Pacific has been estimated to be four times the global average of a 3.2 millimeter rise per year (SPREP 2019).

Increased coral bleaching, as a consequence of ocean acidification, prolonged drought, and erratic rainfall, also threatens the food and water security of the Pacific. Furthermore, extreme weather events like the category 5 cyclones are a common occurrence in the subregion, adversely affecting development gains. A total of 27 category 5 cyclones and 32 category 4 cyclones ravaged the Pacific between 1981 and 2016 (WMO, 2016).

The Pacific is now in a constant state of "recovery and rebuilding" on account of the frequency and the high intensity of the climate-induced disasters it has experienced.

Although disasters triggered by natural hazards are more frequent in the Pacific compared with other regions, there are ways to build resilience to changing climate conditions. Adaptation projects needed to address these risks include climate-proofing of infrastructure, mangrove protection, better water resources management, implementation of early warning systems, and greater uptake of dryland agriculture (IMF 2021b). Table 9 summarizes the climate change priorities for the Pacific countries.

Table 9: Snapshot of Climate Change Priorities in the Pacific, 2018–2019

Country	tCO$_2$e Per Capita in 2020	Net-Zero Target (Year)	LTS/LT Submission	NDC Priority Sectors	NDC Target	Finance Needs	Domestic Public Ependiture on Climate as a Share of National Budget
Cook Islands	2.1 (in 2016)	2040	Not yet submitted	Energy, transport, low-carbon technology, adaptation (marine ecosystem)	Cook Islands' first NDC, submitted in 2016 as Intended NDC Electricity sector target of 38% reduction from 2006 levels, unconditionally by 2020, and −38% by 2030, plus an extra 48% conditionally by 2030	N/A	N/A
Federated States of Micronesia	1.5 (in 2018)	2050	Not yet submitted	Energy, transport, adaptation (coastal protection, climate-resilient agriculture)	Micronesia's first NDC, submitted in 2016 as Intended NDC Unconditional: 28% GHG emission reduction below 2000 level by 2025 Conditional: 35% GHG emission reduction below 2000 level by 2025	N/A	N/A
Fiji	2.5	2050	Net zero in all sectors of economy, particularly transformation in energy and transport system	Energy, transport (land and maritime), adaptation (climate-smart agriculture, built infrastructure, natural resource management)	Republic of Fiji's first NDC (updated submission in 2021) 30% reduction in BAU GHG emissions from the energy sector by 2030 compared with 2013 level	$2.97 billion (2017–2030)	N/A

Continued on next page

Table 9 continued

Country	tCO$_2$e Per Capita in 2020	Net-Zero Target (Year)	LTS/LT Submission	NDC Priority Sectors	NDC Target	Finance Needs	Domestic Public Ependiture on Climate as a Share of National Budget
Kiribati	0.5	2040	Not yet submitted	Energy, transport (sea and land), adaptation (disaster risk management, maritime and coastal sector including mangrove, coastal vegetation and seagrass beds)	Kiribati's first NDC, submitted in 2016 as Intended NDC Unconditional: 13.7% GHG emission reduction by 2025 and 12.8% by 2030 compared with BAU Conditional: 61.8% GHG emission reduction by 2030	$75 million (2013–2023)	N/A
Marshall Islands	2.5	2040	Submitted in Sep 2018: to achieve 100% renewable energy and to facilitates adaptation and climate resilience	Energy, transport (land and sea), waste, adaptation, and climate-resilient agriculture	Marshall Islands' second NDC (updated submission in 2020) 32% GHG emission reduction below 2010 level by 2025, 45% by 2030, and 58% by 2035	N/A	N/A
Nauru	5.2	2040	Not yet submitted	AFOLU, energy, transport, adaptation (water, coastal protection, disaster risk reduction, ecosystem, and biodiversity)	Nauru's first NDC (updated submission in 2021) Unconditional: Implementation of a 6 MW solar PV system Conditional: Improved resilience via transition to untapped clean energy sources, energy efficiency improvement program	Mitigation and adaptation: approximately $85 million, including substantial technical, capacity building, and logistic assistance, given the limited capacity on the island	N/A

Continued on next page

Table 9 continued

Country	tCO$_2$e Per Capita in 2020	Net-Zero Target (Year)	LTS/LT Submission	NDC Priority Sectors	NDC Target	Finance Needs	Domestic Public Ependiture on Climate as a Share of National Budget
Niue	7.0	2040	Not yet submitted	Energy, transport, adaptation (disaster risk reduction, coastal protection)	Niue's first NDC, submitted in 2016 as Intended NDC Unconditional: 38% share of RE in total electricity generation by 2020 Conditional: 80% share of RE in total electricity generation, or even higher levels, by 2025	$10.47 million for energy and energy efficiency sectors up to 2030	N/A
Palau	55.2	2040	Not yet submitted	Energy, transport, waste	Palau's first NDC, submitted in 2016 as Intended NDC 22% energy sector emission reduction below 2005 level by 2025; 45% RE target by 2025; 35% energy efficiency target by 2025	$5.5 million by 2025 for up-front investment cost of renewable energy and energy efficiency	N/A
Papua New Guinea (PNG)	0.8	2040	Not yet submitted	AFOLU (REDD+, forest conservation, sustainable forest management), energy, transport, adaptation (built infrastructure, coastal protection)	PNG's second NDC, submitted in 2020 50% reduction in emissions by 2030, particularly in AFOLU, helping to bridge the global mitigation gap, generating 78% of its electricity supply from renewable energy sources by 2030	$1.37 billion (2020–2030), consisting of $1.2 billion for transport, and $172 million for building and infrastructure	N/A
Samoa	1.8	2040	Not yet submitted	Energy, waste, AFOLU, adaptation (marine, agroforestry, sustainable forestry)	Samoa's second NDC, submitted in 2021 Conditional: 26% emission reduction in 2030, compared with 2007 level	N/A	N/A

Continued on next page

Table 9 continued

Country	tCO$_2$e Per Capita in 2020	Net-Zero Target (Year)	LTS/LT Submission	NDC Priority Sectors	NDC Target	Finance Needs	Domestic Public Ependiture on Climate as a Share of National Budget
Solomon Islands	0.5	2040	Not yet submitted	Energy, AFOLU (carbon storage), adaptation (coastal and marine ecosystem, disaster risk reduction)	Solomon Islands' first NDC (updated submission in 2021) Unconditional: 14% GHG emission reduction below 2015 level by 2025, and 33% GHG emission reduction by 2030, compared with BAU Conditional: Further 27% GHG emission reduction by 2025, and 45% GHG emission reduction by 2030, compared with BAU	$296.75 million (2020–2030), consisting of $170.70 million for mitigation and $126.65 million for national adaptation planning	N/A
Tonga	1.1	2040	Submitted in Nov 2021: 100% renewable electricity by 2035, energy-efficient infrastructure, battery storage facility	Adaptation (marine protected areas), energy, waste, LULUCF	Tonga's second NDC, submitted in 2020 13% energy sector GHG emission reduction by 2030 compared with 2006 level; 70% renewable electricity transition, 30% land used for agroforestry	$83.2 million (2020–2030) for mitigation measures: renewable energy projects	N/A
Tuvalu	0.6	2040	Not yet submitted	Energy, agriculture, waste	Tuvalu's first NDC, submitted in 2016 as Intended NDC 60% GHG emission reduction in energy sector below 2010 level by 2025; 100% reduction in GHG emissions from electricity (power) generation by 100%: almost zero emissions by 2025	$115.23 million (2020–2025) for mitigation measures: renewable electricity and energy efficiency program	N/A

Continued on next page

Table 9 continued

Country	tCO_2e Per Capita in 2020	Net-Zero Target (Year)	LTS/LT Submission	NDC Priority Sectors	NDC Target	Finance Needs	Domestic Public Ependiture on Climate as a Share of National Budget
Vanuatu	0.6	2040	Not yet submitted	Energy, waste, adaptation (marine and forest resource management), LULUCF	Vanuatu's first NDC (updated submission in 2021) Conditional: Transition to close to 100% renewable energy in electricity generation sector by 2030	$173.6 million (2020–2030) for mitigation measures	N/A

AFOLU = agriculture, forestry, and land use; BAU = business as usual; GHG = greenhouse gas; LTS = long-term strategy; LULUCF = land use, land-use change, and forestry; NDC = Nationally Determined Contribution; RE = renewable energy; tCO_2e = metric tons of carbon dioxide equivalent.

Note: N/A = data not available. In this table's last column, the reference is to the absence of disclosed information on domestic public expenditure on climate-related activities and projects as a share of the national budget.

Source: UNFCCC's NDC Registry.

4.5.2 Subregional Landscape and Key Trends

Climate finance in the Pacific in 2018–2019 amounted to $1.4 billion, or 0.3% of total tracked finance in this report. Solomon Islands, Papua New Guinea (PNG), and Tonga were the top-three recipients of climate finance in the Pacific subregion, at 18% ($240 million), 14% ($198 million), and 9% ($122 million) of the Pacific climate finance total, respectively. Climate finance was accessed either directly through bilateral donors and multilateral development banks or through multilateral climate funds.

Even though many stakeholders were involved in providing finance, the current volume was not enough to meet the NDC financing target of $5.2 billion. For adaptation alone, the Pacific needed about 9% of average annual GDP, or almost $1 billion, for building coastal protection infrastructure (IMF 2021b).

Financing sources. The Pacific received strong public climate finance support of $1.3 billion for 2018 and 2019 (or 97% of total climate finance in the Pacific). Public international finance was the primary source of Pacific climate finance. Multilateral DFIs, international climate and public funds, and foreign governments provided a total of $442 million (or 32% of the total climate finance), $406 million (30%), and $402 million (30%), respectively, in the 2-year period. The GCF was the largest provider of multilateral climate finance, while Australia, New Zealand, European Union, and Japan have led the way in bilateral climate support for the Pacific.

Private finance ($61 million), representing 4% of total Pacific climate finance, was contributed by corporations ($56 million, or 9 3% of total private finance) and the rest by commercial financial institutions ($5 million, or 7% of total private finance), mainly to support energy and building and infrastructure projects. Private sector investments were provided as sustainability funding through microfinance institutions and aid-funded programs. The former included the South Pacific Business Development (SPBD) network, which is active in Fiji, Samoa, Solomon Islands, Tonga, and Vanuatu, and VANWODS Microfinance, operating in Vanuatu. Recently it also included the IFC Pacific Microfinance Initiative and the New Zealand Official Development Assistance–funded Business Link Pacific; both are active throughout the Pacific.

Sectors financed. The Pacific received about equal portions of mitigation, adaptation, and dual-benefit finance, reaching total flows of $456 million, $460 million, and $449 million, r espectively, in 2018–2019. This finance was directed toward the energy and transport sectors, totaling $529 million (39% of the total), followed by the waste and water sectors, totaling $165.5 million (12% of the total). Almost half of adaptation finance was sourced from multilateral DFIs (43% of adaptation finance, or $198 million), clima te funds (mainly GCF and GEF; 40% of adaptation finance, or $184 million), the government budget (16% of adaptation finance, or $75 million), and bilateral DFIs (1% of adaptation finance, or $3 million). Adaptation finance mainly targeted biodiversity, land and marine conservation, DRM, and policy support and capacity building.

Climate finance with both mitigation and adaptation benefits was also relatively high compared with other regions. Two-thirds of dual-benefit finance ($539 million, or 39% of the total) comprised cross-sector finance, such as low-carbon technology supporting power generation, land use, and natural resource management. Figure 24 shows the breakdown of the use of climate finance the Pacific subregion.

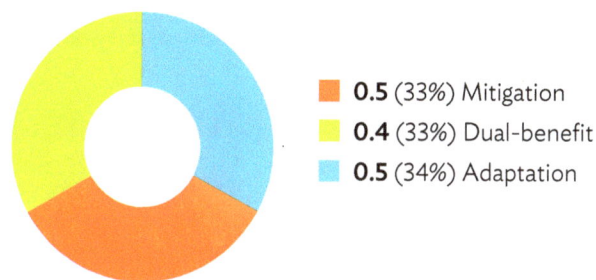

Figure 24: Mitigation and Adaptation Finance in the Pacific Subregion, 2018–2019
($ billion)

- **0.5** (33%) Mitigation
- **0.4** (33%) Dual-benefit
- **0.5** (34%) Adaptation

Source: Authors' compilation.

Financing instruments. Almost all climate adaptation projects in the Pacific have been financed through grants, accounting for 72% ($980 million) of the Pacific climate finance in 2018–2019 (Figure 25). The grants were channeled mainly through public climate funds (41%), government budget (37%), multilateral DFIs (21%), and bilateral DFIs (2%). Of the grant total, 46% went to cross-sector investments; 26%, to AFOLU; and 13%, to waste and water.

Debt instruments represented 26% of total Pacific climate finance, or $357 million. More than half (64%) of total debt was provided at low-cost project debt to finance energy, transport, and cross-sector projects, by multilateral and bilateral DFIs. Solomon Islands has used concessional loans under a $70 million, 40-year loan, for a GCF-cofinanced hydropower project. Papua New Guinea and Tonga have also received concessional loans, but in smaller amounts (IMF 2021b). Market-rate project-level debt (26% of total debt) was contributed mainly by SOEs, government, and multilateral DFIs. Meanwhile, balance-sheet debt financing was provided by corporations and commercial financial institutions. Corporations also provided $28 million in balanc e-sheet equity financing, accounting for 2% of total Pacific climate finance, to support renewable energy generation and its infrastructure.

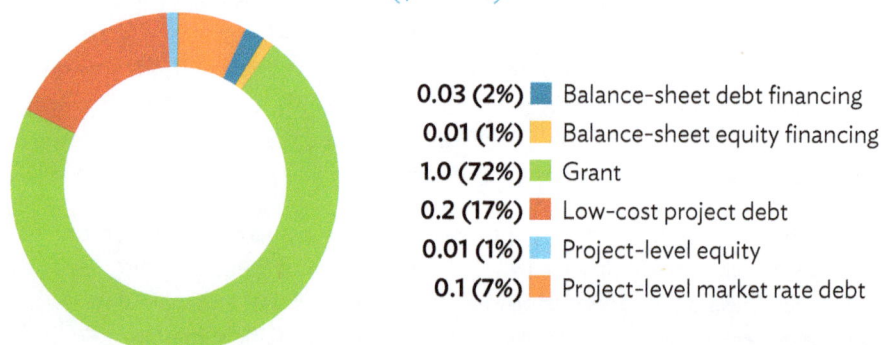

Figure 25: Breakdown of Climate Finance Instruments in the Pacific, 2018–2019
($ billion)

- 0.03 (2%) ▄ Balance-sheet debt financing
- 0.01 (1%) ▄ Balance-sheet equity financing
- 1.0 (72%) ▄ Grant
- 0.2 (17%) ▄ Low-cost project debt
- 0.01 (1%) ▄ Project-level equity
- 0.1 (7%) ▄ Project-level market rate debt

Source: Authors' compilation.

Impact of COVID-19 on climate finance flow. COVID-19 massively affected the whole economy of the Pacific. GDP growth contracted to –6% in 2020. Furthermore, because of the mobility restrictions applied during the pandemic, the cost of shipping went up, increasing the cost of various equipment and other supplies and causing delays in projects.

The Pacific's case was unique compared with that of other subregions: it secured a variety of approved international financing commitments from multilateral DFIs and climate funds. For instance, the GCF funding agreement stipulated that any contract with costs that were more than 10% higher than those initially approved had to be individually reviewed. Countries with approved funding would experience delays in disbursement, resulting in a wider climate funding gap.

COVID-19 also influenced investor activity and attitudes, as evidenced by the slower rate of private investment. ADB estimates that the total cost of climate change, which covers economic, social, and environment aspects in the Pacific, could reach up to 12.7% of annual GDP by 2100.[15]

Gap analysis. Accurately estimating the financial cost of climate change in the Pacific was challenging, given the degree of risks and uncertainty associated with climate change. The annual financing need for adaptation activities up to 2040 has been estimated at 9% of GDP, or $1 billion (IMF 2021a; Atteridge and Canales 2017). However, the current state of adaptation finance is far below the required needs: the The Global Landscape (CPI 2019a) acknowledged a total of only $460 million in adaptation finance in 2018–2019. Furthermore, a very minimum amount of finance in the Pacific was tracked, particularly from the national budget (less than 1% of Pacific climate finance). This indicates the lack of climate finance availability and climate data disclosure from government, and highlights the importance of strengthening national policies in climate finance tracking and tagging.

4.5.3 Challenges and Opportunities

Some Pacific countries are located remotely from major global markets; mobilizing climate finance is not only challenging, but also costly (Maclellan and Meads 2016). One-third of climate finance provided to the Pacific was for mitigation activities, in the shorter term, if compared with adaptation projects, which required longer-term finance and implementation. Bilateral sources accommodate more urgent climate projects, as bilaterally funded projects tend to be disbursed more quickly with fewer or more tailored access requirements that take

---

[15] The estimate excluded the cost of rare but catastrophic events such as category 5 cyclones, which have been observed recently in the Pacific.

country-specific conditions into account. On the other hand, multilateral climate finance, including large global funds like the GCF, is increasingly needed to support adaptation projects, given the sizable financing requirements. So far, the Pacific has accessed global climate funds through international or regional accredited entities.

The process of accessing multilateral climate funds has proven to be complex and to involve a longer time to complete because of limited institutional capacity (Samuwai 2021). To be perceived as "ready," recipient countries must first exhibit a reasonable degree of knowledge to navigate the international climate finance environment, identify funding sources, and prepare the required ecosystem (capacity, institutions, systems, and processes) to meet the robust fiduciary standards set by international financiers (Samuwai and Hills 2018). Fiji and the Cook Islands are the only two countries in the Pacific that have attained national accreditation with the GCF. The Micronesia Conservation Trust, the Secretariat of the Pacific Regional Environment Programme, and the Pacific Community function as subregional accredited entities. The adaptation projects typically take several years from start to completion, with heightened environmental and social safeguards and inclusion of gender policies (IMF 2021a).

Global climate finance flows are mitigation-centric, with the private sector as the main financing source. This subregion needs more adaptation measures, but existing private investments in the Pacific are primarily geared toward renewable energy, with minimum involvement in adaptation opportunities. Access to adaptation finance is very competitive, and most funding goes to the larger Asian countries, which tend to have higher institutional capacity and larger projects. There are, however, opportunities to scale up and redirect climate finance for adaptation in the Pacific (Box 5).

4.5.4 Case Study: Exploring various Financing Mechanisms to fill the Adaptation Finance Gap

All the Pacific countries are committed to reaching net-zero carbon emissions by 2050, despite their small contribution to global GHG emissions. Out of the 14 countries in the subregion, 8 have submitted their updated first NDC or second NDC, committing themselves to working toward more ambitious climate goals. These goals include: (i) a larger emission reduction target for mitigation actions, through an increased share for renewable energy in power generation and through economy-wide energy efficiency; and (ii) heightened climate adaptation action, including DRM, coastal protection, and waste and water management.

For example, the Government of Fiji has prepared its high-level strategic National Adaptation Plan, containing the 160 adaptation measures identified as the most urgent, to be implemented over a 5-year period. In 2021, the Fiji Parliament approved the country's Climate Change Act, setting the legal framework for its climate-related and DRM actions, such as establishing (i) its NZE target by 2050 in its long-term emission reduction target; and (ii) its ocean sustainability target, defining territorial seas to be 100% sustainably and effectively managed, and an exclusive economic zone be designated as a marine protected area, by 2030. Because of its more ambitious targets, Fiji continues to excel at implementing a wide range of financial instruments in climate pipelines, redirecting finance toward adaptation, and attract more private sector participation. The financing instruments used are as follows:

- **Environment and climate adaptation levy**, designed in 2017–2018 as a consortium of taxes on prescribed services, items, and income (Table 10), to support natural environment protection, reduction of the carbon footprint, and adaptation of the economy, communities, and infrastructure to climate change impact. The government has managed to raise FJ$270.2 million ($118 million) through the environment and climate adaptation levy (ECAL) revenues; F$255.9 million ($93 million) of this amount was used to finance 102 climate change and environmental conservation projects through the national budget, as well as to support the launching of the Climate Change Relocation Trust Fund (Ministry of Economy, Fiji, 2019).[16] ECAL has proven to be a steady source of government revenue to support Fiji's climate change adaptation efforts.

Table 10: Environment and Climate Adaptation Levy in Fiji—Coverage and Rates, 2018–2019

Particulars	Rate
Luxury vehicles	10% tax on imports
Miscellaneous super-yacht charters and docking fees	10% charge
Individuals earning more than F$270,000 ($124,000) a year	10% of income tax
Plastic bags	F$0.20 ($0.10)
Businesses with turnover of F$1.5 million ($680,000) a year	10% of prescribed services offered

Source: Ministry of Economy, Fiji (2019).

- **Tailor-made insurance products catering to the specific needs of climate projects in Fiji or other Pacific countries** were introduced in 2017, to encourage more private sector participation by balancing the risks and opportunities associated with the project. These products were designed to capture scalable finance with a more flexible requirement that meets specific country/project requirements.

- **Grants and concessional loans via direct access to international climate funds, through accreditation.** The Fiji National Development Bank was accredited with the GCF in 2017 as part of the government's strategy of climate-proof infrastructure development and increased economic resilience (Fiji Development Bank 2018). The bank was categorized as a "micro entity" that could access only up to $10 million in GCF project funding, in the form of loans, equity, and guarantees. In 2020, the GCF approved 50% c ofinancing for FDB's first mitigation project, worth $10 million (GCF 2021).

Despite these efforts to channel climate finance flows, the scale of investments needed for full NDC target achievement surpassed Fiji's current capacity to finance such a transformational environment. Compared with bigger economies like East Asia and Southeast Asia, the Pacific had a capital market that was still developing, and encountering difficulties in attracting green and climate-related funding because of the relatively small pool of investors, and limited climate finance capacity and knowledge. There was also a lack of investment vehicles to cater to private financers, such as private equities and venture capital funds. In the case of Fiji, the Fiji Investment Corporation had been set up to accommodate a private investment pool, but it continued to struggle with poor returns and delinquency. Meanwhile, banks were still geared mainly for the better-developed sectors of the economy, such as tourism, manufacturing, agriculture, and real estate.

---

[16] The Climate Change Relocation Trust Fund was designed to assist the government in dealing with the cost of relocating communities in response to the impact of climate change and as a mechanism for channeling international donor support for Fiji's adaptation efforts (Government of Fiji 2019). The fund is still not yet operational.

Box 7: Fiji's Subregional Learning and Sharing as an Effort to Close the Knowledge and Capacity Gap in the Pacific for Climate Finance Readiness

The Government of Fiji, with other Pacific member countries (Kiribati, the Marshall Islands, Samoa, Solomon Islands, Tonga, Tuvalu, and Vanuatu), joined the Climate Finance Readiness for the Pacific (CFRP) Project of the Pacific Islands Forum Secretariat. Their main objective in joining the program was to identify key areas within the public financial management system that needed strengthening, in order to gain access to global climate finance sources.

In 2017, Fiji Development Bank obtained National Implementing Entity (NIE) accreditation with the Green Climate Fund (GCF). That same year, the government was accredited as NIE with the Adaptation Fund and successfully secured $4.2 million in adaptation project financing, aimed at increasing the resilience of informal urban settlements in Fiji that were highly vulnerable to climate change and disaster risks (Adaptation Fund 2021).

Fiji shared its successful past experience within the Pacific Islands Forum, for others to learn from. The sharing session was part of a peer-to-peer learning platform aimed at studying Fiji's process of accreditation as NIE with the GCF and the Adaptation Fund. The peer-to-peer learning took place in 2020 to strengthen and consolidate climate finance knowledge and expertise across the Pacific Forum region.

The Government of Tuvalu made the most of this experience, and also attained NIE accreditation with the Adaptation Fund. Mirroring Fiji's strategy, Tuvalu improved its climate finance consolidation and reporting of the Tuvalu Development Fund under the Official Development Assistance Framework, in accordance with the partners'/funders' requirements.

The CFRP Project, a two-way learning experience, benefited Fiji through collaborative knowledge sharing. It provided the Pacific member countries with an opportuninty to share techniques and processes for integrating climate finance into their country's public financial management system.

Appendix

Table A1: Asia and the Pacific Climate Finance, 2018–2019, by Sector and Subsector
($ million)

Sector/Subsector	2018	2019	Total
Water and wastewater management	5,963	12,079	18,042
Disaster risk management	7,563	6,858	14,421
AFOLU and natural resource management	2,333	1,268	3,601
Infrastructure, energy, and other built environment	502	1,625	2,127
Adaptation cross-sectoral	907	779	1,687
Policy, national budget support, and capacity building	240	415	655
Industry, extractive industries, manufacturing, and trade	161	64	225
Total, Adaptation finance	**17,669**	**23,088**	**40,757**
Energy systems	122,691	132,951	255,642
Low-carbon transport	73,477	116,173	189,649
Buildings and infrastructure	-	10,946	10,946
AFOLU and fisheries	5,079	4,576	9,654
Mitigation cross-sectoral	2,397	2,609	5,006
Industry	-	585	585
Policy and national budget support and capacity building	235	342	577
Waste	47	343	390
Low-carbon technologies	6	-	6
Total, Mitigation finance	**203,932**	**267,915**	**472,457**
Total, Dual benefit finance	**3,984**	**2,708**	**6,692**
Grand total	**225,585**	**293,711**	**519,906**

AFOLU = Agriculture, forestry, and other land use

Table A2: Asia and the Pacific Climate Finance, 2018–2019, by Recipient Subregion and Country
($ million)

Country/Subregion	2018	2019	Total	Population (2021)
Armenia	107	114	222	2,974,272
Azerbaijan	66	123	190	10,324,162
Georgia	282	604	886	3,974,050
Kazakhstan	706	1.311	2,017	18,776,707
Kyrgyz Republic	112	172	283	6,524,195
Pakistan	2,647	2,959	5,606	220,892,340
Tajikistan	130	244	374	9,537,645
Turkmenistan	5	5	10	6,031,200
Uzbekistan	1,034	1,534	2,568	33,469,203
Cross-Central and West Asia developing countries*	72	177	248	
Total, Central and West Asia	**5,160**	**7,244**	**12,405**	**312,503,774**
People's Republic of China	170,585	246,339	416,924	1,439,323,776
Mongolia	532	602	1,134	3,278,290
Total, East Asia	**171,117**	**246,941**	**418,058**	**1,442,602,066**
Cook Islands	7	4	10	17,596
Federated States of Micronesia	26	36	62	559,907
Fiji	39	44	83	896,445
Kiribati	30	34	64	119,449
Marshall Islands	12	54	66	59,190
Nauru	25	29	54	10,824
Niue	2	1	2	1,648
Palau	49	2	51	18,094
Papua New Guinea	109	89	198	8,947,024
Samoa	45	37	82	201,067
Solomon Islands	40	199	240	686,884

Continued on next page

Table A2 continued

Country/Subregion	2018	2019	Total	Population (2021)
Tonga	89	33	122	108,113
Tuvalu	23	21	44	12,089
Vanuatu	24	30	54	307,145
Cross-Pacific developing countries**	88	145	233	
Total, Pacific	**608**	**757**	**1,365**	**11,945,475**
Bangladesh	3,373	2,750	6,123	164,689,383
Bhutan	9	41	50	771,608
India	21,058	17,539	38,597	1,380,004,385
Maldives	7	21	28	540,544
Nepal	370	508	878	29,136,808
Sri Lanka	87	1,053	1,140	21,413,249
Total, South Asia	**24,904**	**21,912**	**46,816**	**1,596,555,977**
Cambodia	439	1,096	1,535	16,718,965
Indonesia	4,403	2,252	6,655	273,523,615
Lao People's Democratic Republic (Lao PDR)	101	269	370	7,275,560
Philippines	3,205	5,512	8,718	109,581,078
Thailand	1,047	622	1,669	69,799,978
Timor-Leste	13	88	101	1,318,445
Viet Nam	4,797	4,002	8,799	97,338,579
Total, Southeast Asia	**14,006**	**13,841**	**27,846**	**575,556,220**
Total, Transregional*	**9,789**	**3,627**	**13,416**	
Grand Total	**225,584**	**294,322**	**519,906**	**3,939,163,512**
Grand Total	**225,584**	**294,322**	**519,906**	

*Cross-Central and West Asia developing countries consist of finances that are used for climate-related projects and programs in several Central and West
Asian developing countries. Due to limitation in our data granularity, this "cross-countries" amount cannot be further separated per country-level.
**Cross-Pacific developing countries consist of finances that are used for climate-related projects and programs in several Pacific developing countries. Due to limitation in our data granularity, this amount cannot be further separated per country-level.
***Transregional covered the finance flow associated with one or more of the five subregions in Asia and the Pacific. All source of finance came from public sector, mainly to finance mitigation targeting energy and low-carbon transport, as well as cross-sectors (e.g. building and infrastructure, industry, water and wastewater, and AFOLU).
AFOLU = agriculture, forestry, and other land use.
Source: Authors' compilation.

Table A3: Asia and the Pacific Climate Finance, 2018–2019, by Financing Source

Financing Source	2018	2019	Total
Corporations	42,334	29,971	72,305
Households/Individuals	25,014	22,749	47,763
Commercial financial institutions	14,613	30,464	45,077
Funds	516	1,035	1,551
Institutional Investors	1,052	259	1,311
Unknown		43	43
Total, Private financing	**83,529**	**84,521**	**168,050**
National DFIs	66,230	124,835	191,064
Government budget and agencies	48,413	58,608	107,021
Multilateral DFIs	13,135	16,226	29,361
Bilateral DFIs	12,902	8,371	21,272
Multilateral climate funds	834	961	1,795
Export credit agencies (ECAs)	314	555	869
Public funds	227	246	473
Total, Public Financing	**142,055**	**209,802**	**351,856**
Grand Total	**225,584**	**294,323**	**519,906**
Grand Total based on Given Figures	**225,584**	**294,323**	**519,906**

DFI = Development financial institution

Table A4: Asia and the Pacific Climate Finance, 2018–2019, by Financing Instrument
($ million)

Financing instrument	2018	2019	Total
Project-level market rate debt	104,963	159,666	264,629
Balance sheet debt financing	31,702	4,534	76,236
Low-cost project debt	15,277	9,628	24,905
Balance sheet equity financing	48,115	53,905	102,020
Project-level equity	11,285	13,940	25,225
Grant	12,294	12,611	24,905
Others	1,947	39	1,986
Grand Total	**225,583**	**246,323**	**519,906**

Source: Authors' compilation.

Table A5: Asia and the Pacific Climate Finance Needs up to 2030
($ billion)

Country	Status of NDC document	Average per year Mitigation + Adapatation — Financing needs conditional up to 2030	Total Mitigation + Adapatation — Financing needs conditional up to 2030	Notes
Armenia	First, updated	na	na	
Azerbaijan	INDC	na	na	
Georgia	First, updated	na	na	
Kazakhstan	INDC (submitted as First NDC)	na	na	
Kyrgyz Republic	First, updated	1.0	10.0	
Pakistan	First, updated	16.6	16.0	
Tajikistan	First, updated	1.0	10.0	
Turkmenistan**	First, updated		na	
Uzbekistan	First, updated			
Cross-Central and West Asia				
Total, Central and West Asia		**18.6**	**36.0**	

Continued on next page

Table A5 continued

Country	Status of NDC document	Average per year Mitigation + Adapatation Financing needs conditional up to 2030	Total Mitigation + Adapatation Financing needs conditional up to 2030	Notes
PRC	First, updated	1,400.0	14,000.0	
Mongolia	First, updated	1.3	12.5	
Total, East Asia		**1,401.3**	**14,012.5**	
Cook Islands	First	na	na	
Federated States of Micronesia	First, updated		na	
Fiji	First, updated	0.3	2.9	
Kiribati*	INDC	0.03	0.08	up to 2023
Marshall Islands	Second, updated			
Nauru	First, updated		0.09	
Niue	INDC	0.001	0.01	up to 2020
Palau	INDC	0.001	0.01	up to 2025
Papua New Guinea	Second	0.1	1.4	
Samoa	Second		na	
Solomon Islands	First, updated	0.03	0.3	
Tonga	Second	0.01	0.08	
Tuvalu	First, updated	0.02	0.1	up to 2025
Vanuatu	First, updated	0.02	0.2	
Cross-Pacific				
Total, Pacific		**0.54**	**5.17**	

Continued on next page

Table A5 continued

Country	Status of NDC document	Average per year Mitigation + Adapatation — Financing needs conditional up to 2030	Total Mitigation + Adapatation — Financing needs conditional up to 2030	Notes
Bangladesh	First, updated	19.5	195.1	
Bhutan	Second	0.4	3.5	
India	INDC	250.0	2,500.0	
Maldives	First, updated	na	na	
Nepal	Second	2.50	25.0	
Sri Lanka		0.4	3.9	NDC financing need is calculated based on estimated loss and damage from climate change
Total, South Asia		**272.8**	**2,727.5**	
Cambodia	First; updated	0.8	7.8	
Indonesia	First; updated	2.4	23.9	
Lao PDR	First; updated	0.1	0.5	
Philippines	First	0.09	0.9	NDC financing need is calculated based on estimated loss and damage from climate change
Thailand	Second, updated	na	na	
Timor-Leste	First, updated	na	na	
Viet Nam	First; updated	3.5	35.0	
Total, Southeast Asia		**6.89**	**68.1**	
Grand total		**1,699.9**	**16,999.3**	

INDC = Intended Nationally Determined Contribution; n.a = data is not available NDC = Nationally Determined Contribution.
Note: First=INDCs submitted or considered as first NDCs (e.g., Cook Islands) and NDCs submitted as first NDCs (e.g., Philippines); Second = Second NDC submissions; Updated = updated versions of current active NDC submissions.
* India submitted its Updated First NDC on 26 August 2022.
** Turkmenistan and Kiribati submitted their updated NDC on 31 January and 2 March 2023, while this r eport was completed in 2022.
Source: Authors' estimates based on investment needs for climate change mitigation or adaptation, or both, in accordance with the commitments made by 38 developing countries in their NDCs

Table A6: Climate Finance by Development Finance Institution (DFI)
($ billion)

Mitigation	2018	2019	Total
Bilateral DFIs	10.86	5.99	16.85
Multilateral DFIs	6.58	10.06	16.64
National DFIs	54.85	110.36	165.21
Total, Mitigation finance	**72.29**	**126.41**	**198.70**
Bilateral DFIs	1.39	1.96	3.36
Multilateral DFIs	4.15	5.25	9.40
National DFIs	11.38	14.47	25.86
Total, Adaptation finance	**16.92**	**21.69**	**38.61**
Grand total	**89.21**	**148.10**	**237.31**
Grand Total based on Given Figures	**89.21**	**148.10**	**237.31**

DFI = development finance institution.
Source: Authors' compilation.

References

Acharya, M., J. Sinha, S. Jain, and R. Padmanabhi. 2020. Landscape of Green Finance in India. San Francisco: Climate Policy Initiative. https://www.climatepolicyinitiative.org/wp-content/uploads/2020/09/Landscape-of-Green-Finance-in-India-1-2.pdf.

Adaptation Fund. 2021. *Increasing the resilience of informal urban settlements in Fiji that are highly vulnerable to climate change and disaster risks.* https://www.adaptation-fund.org/project/increasing-resilience-informal-urban-settlements-fiji-highly-vulnerable-climate-change-disaster-risks-2/.

African Development Bank Group (AfDB), Asian Development Bank (ADB), Asian Infrastructure Investment Bank (AIIB), European Bank for Reconstruction and Development (EBRD), European Investment Bank (EIB), Inter-American Development Bank Group (IDBG), Islamic Development Bank (IsDB), New Development Bank (NDB), and World Bank Group (WBG). 2018a. *Lessons Learned from Three Years of Implementing the MDB-IDFC Common Principles for Climate Change Adaptation Finance Tracking.* London. https://www.idfc.org/wp-content/uploads/2018/12/mdb_idfc_lessonslearned-full-report.pdf.

—————.2018b. *MDBs' Alignment Approach to the Objectives of the Paris Agreement: Working Together to Catalyse Low-Emissions and Climate-Resilient Development.* London. https://thedocs.worldbank.org/en/doc/784141543806348331-0020022018/original/JointDeclarationMDBsAlignmentApproachtoParisAgreementCOP24Final.pdf.

—————.2021. 2020 *Joint Report on Multilateral Development Banks' Climate Finance.* London. https://thedocs.worldbank.org/en/doc/9234bfc633439d0172f6a6eb8df1b881-0020012021/original/2020-Joint-MDB-report-on-climate-finance-Report-final-web.pdf.

Alcayna, T. 2020. *At What Cost? How Chronic Gaps in Adaptation Finance Expose the World's Poorest People to Climate Chaos.* Zurich Flood Resilience Alliance. https://floodresilience.net/resources/item/at-what-cost-how-chronic-gaps-in-adaptation-finance-expose-the-world-s-poorest-people-to-climate-chaos/.

Amerasinghe, N. M., J. Thwaites, G. Larsen, and A. Ballesteros. 2017. *The Future of the Funds: Exploring the Architecture of Multilateral Climate Finance.* Washington, DC: World Resources Institute. https://www.wri.org/research/future-funds-exploring-architecture-multilateral-climate-finance.

Aon. 2019. *Weather, Climate & Catastrophe Insight: 2018 Annual Report.* Dublin. https://www.aon.com/getmedia/c0d16c46-4a8d-4390-b233-5a705977be32/20190122-ab-if-annual-weather-climate-report-2018.pdf.

ASEAN Coordinating Centre for Humanitarian Assistance on Disaster Management (AHA Centre). 2022. ASEAN Weekly Disaster Updates Week 23 and Week 24. Jakarta. https://ahacentre.org/weekly-disaster-update/weekly-disaster-update-6-12-june-2022.

—————.2022. ASEAN Weekly Disaster Updates Week 24. Jakarta. https://ahacentre.org/wp-content/uploads/2022/06/DWeek_24_13-19Jun2022.pdf.

Asian Development Bank (ADB). n.d. Mongolia : Managing Solid Waste in Secondary Cities.
https://www.adb.org/projects/52303-001/main.

————.n.d. Japan Fund for Poverty Reduction. https://www.adb.org/multimedia/jfpr-2022/.

————.2012. *Technical Assistance for the Economics of Climate Change in Central and West Asia (Cofinanced by the Climate Change Fund and the Asia Clean Energy Fund under the Clean Energy Financing Partnership Facility).* Manila.

————.2014. Climate Change May Slash 9% from South Asia's Economy by 2100 – Report. *News release.* 19 August.

————.2017. *Southeast Asia Green Recovery Can Create More Than 30 Million Jobs by 2030—ADB.* https://www.adb.org/news/southeast-asia-green-recovery-can-create-more-30-million-jobs-2030-adb.

————.2019. *Ending Hunger in Asia and the Pacific by 2030: An Assessment in Investment Requirements in Agriculture.* https://www.adb.org/sites/default/files/publication/533281/ending-hunger-asia-pacific-2030.pdf.

————.2020. ADB Accelerating Renewable Energy in Mongolia with Advanced Battery Storage System. *News Release.* 24 April.
https://www.adb.org/news/adb-accelerating-renewable-energy-mongolia-advanced-battery-storage-system.

————.2021a. Asian Development Bank and Mongolia: Fact Sheet. Manila. https://www.adb.org/sites/default/files/publication/27781/mon-2021.pdf.

————.2021b. Asian Development Bank and the People's Republic of China: Fact Sheet. Manila. https://www.adb.org/sites/default/files/publication/27789/prc-2021.pdf.

————.2021c. Climate Risk Country Profile: Indonesia. Manila: ADB. https://www.adb.org/sites/default/files/publication/700411/climate-risk-country-profile-indonesia.pdf.

————.2021d. *Energy Efficiency in South Asia: Opportunities for Energy Sector Transformation.* Manila. https://www.adb.org/sites/default/files/publication/761251/energy-efficiency-south-asia-opportunities.pdf.

————.2021e. Partners Pledge $665 Million to Support Green Recovery in ASEAN. *News release.* 2 November. https://www.adb.org/news/partners-pledge-665-million-support-green-recovery-asean.

————.2022. *Where We Work. Manila.* https://www.adb.org/where-we-work/main. (accessed 28 February 2022).

Atteridge, A., and N. Canales. 2017. Climate Finance in the Pacific: An Overview of Flows to the Region's Small Island Developing States. *Working Paper* 2017-04. Stockholm Environment Institute. https://www.greengrowthknowledge.org/sites/default/files/downloads/resource/SEI-WP-2017-04-Pacific-climate-finance-flows.pdf.

Aylward-Mills, D., J. Payne, M. Sudirman, M. E. Wijaya, B. M. Mecca, M. Zeki, and A. R. Haesra. 2021. *Improving the Impact of Fiscal Stimulus in Asia: An Analysis of Green Recovery Investments and Opportunities.* Climate Policy Initiative and Vivid Economics. https://www.climatepolicyinitiative.org/wp-content/uploads/2021/02/Improving-the-impact-of-fiscal-stimulus-in-Asia.pdf.

Barnard, S., S. Nakhooda, A. Caravani, and L. Schalatek. 2015. Climate Finance Regional Briefing: Asia. *Climate Finance Fundamentals.* 8 (December). London: Heinrich Böll Stiftung North America and Overseas Development Institute. https://us.boell.org/sites/default/files/uploads/2015/11/cff8_2015_eng_asia.pdf.

Biodiversity Finance Initiative (BIOFIN) – UNDP. 2019. *Overview of Public and Private Expenditures on Environmental Protection in the Kyrgyz Republic with Focus on Biodiversity and Climate Adaptation.* Brussels. https://www.undp.org/sites/g/files/zskgke326/files/migration/kg/UNDP_Obzor_Block_en.pdf.

Bloomberg New Energy Finance (BNEF). 2021. *Energy Transition Investment Trends 2021 – Tracking Global Investment in the Low-Carbon Energy Transition.* London. https://assets.bbhub.io/professional/sites/24/Energy-Transition-Investment-Trends_Free-Summary_Jan2021.pdf.

Brown, J., and I. Granoff. 2018. *Deep Decarbonization by 2050: Rethinking the Role of Climate Finance.* San Francisco: Climate Policy Initiative. https://www.climatepolicyinitiative.org/wp-content/uploads/2018/07/Deep-decarbonization-by-2050-rethinking-the-role-of-climate-finance.pdf.

Central Bank of Mongolia. 2021. *About Green Loans:* Quarter 4. https://www.mongolbank.mn/eng/liststatistic.aspx?id=21.

Choi, J., and T. C. Heller. 2021. *The Potential for Scaling Climate Finance in China.* San Francisco: Climate Policy Initiative. https://www.climatepolicyinitiative.org/wp-content/uploads/2021/02/The-Potential-for-Scaling-Climate-Finance-in-China-1.pdf.

Clar, C. 2019. Coordinating Climate Change Adaptation across Levels of Government: The Gap between Theory and Practice of Integrated Adaptation Strategy Processes. *Journal of Environmental Planning and Management.* (12, O ctober). pp. 2166–2185. https://doi.org/10.1080/09640568.2018.1536604.

Climate Analytics. 2019 *Decarbonising South and South East Asia: Shifting energy supply in South Asia and South East Asia to non-fossil fuel-based energy systems in line with the Paris Agreement long-term temperature goal and achievement of Sustainable Development Goals.* https://climateanalytics.org/media/decarbonisingasia2019-fullreport-climateanalytics.pdf.

Climate Action Tracker. 2021. Glasgow's 2030 Credibility Gap: Net Zero's Lip Service to Climate Action. Cologne. https://climateactiontracker.org/publications/glasgows-2030-credibility-gap-net-zeros-lip-service-to-climate-action/.

Climate Finance Group for Latin America and the Caribbean (GFLAC) and United Nations Development Programme (UNDP). 2018. *A Review of Domestic Data Sources for Climate Finance Flows in Recipient Countries.* New York. https://www.undp.org/sites/g/files/zskgke326/files/migration/asia_pacific_rbap/RBAP-DG-2018-Review-of-Domestic-Data-Sources-for-Climate-Finance-Flows.pdf.

Climate Funds Update (CFU). 2021. *Climate Finance Thematic Briefing: Adaptation Finance.* Prepared by C. Watson and L. Schalatek. https://climatefundsupdate.org/wp-content/uploads/2021/03/CFF3-ENG-2020-Digital.pdf.

Climate Policy Initiative (CPI). 2019a. *Global Landscape of Climate Finance 2019.* Prepared by B. Buchner, A. Clark, A. Falconer, R. Macquarie, C. Meattle, R. Tolentino, and C. Wetherbee San Francisco.

————.2019b. *Global Landscape of Climate Finance 2019: Methodology.* San Francisco. http://climatepolicyinitiative.org/wp-content/uploads/2019/11/GLCF-2019-Methodology-Document.pdf.

————.2020. *Updated View on the Global Landscape of Climate Finance 2019.* Prepared by R. Macquarie, B. Naran, P. Rosane, M. Solomon, C. Wetherbee. San Fransisco. https://www.climatepolicyinitiative.org/wp-content/uploads/2020/12/Updated-View-on-the-2019-Global-Landscape-of-Climate-Finance.pdf.

————.2021. *Global Landscape of Climate Finance 2021: Preview.* Prepared by B. Naran, P. Fernandes, R. Padmanabhi, P. Rosane, M. Solomon, S. Stout, C. Strinati, R. Tolentino, E. Wakaba, Y. Zhu, and B. Buchner. San Francisco. https://www.climatepolicyinitiative.org/wp-content/uploads/2021/10/Global-Landscape-of-Climate-Finance-2021.pdf.

Coalition of Finance Ministers for Climate Action. 2020. *Climate Budget Scenario of Bangladesh.* Washington, DC: World Bank. https://www.financeministersforclimate.org/sites/cape/files/inline-files/Session%202%20-%20Bangladesh%20Writeup.pdf.

Day, S., Forster, T., Himmelsbach, J., Korte, L., Mucke, P., Radtke, K., Thielburger, P., Weller, D. 2019. World Risk Report 2019. Bündnis Entwicklung Hilft and Ruhr University Bochum. https://weltrisikobericht.de/wp-content/uploads/2019/09/WorldRiskReport-2019_Online_english.pdf.

Eckstein, D., V. Künzel, and L. Schäfer. 2021. *Global Climate Risk Index 2021: Who Suffers Most from Extreme Weather Events? Weather-Related Loss Events in 2019 and 2000–2019.* Bonn: Germanwatch. https://germanwatch.org/sites/default/files/Global%20Climate%20Risk%20Index%202021_1.pdf.

Eckstein, D., Künzel, V., Schäfer, L., Winges, M. 2020. *Global Climate Risk Index 2020: Who Suffers Most from Extreme Weather Events? Weather-Related Loss Events in 2018 and 1999 to 2018.* Bonn: Germanwatch. https://www.germanwatch.org/sites/default/files/20-2-01e%20Global%20Climate%20Risk%20Index%202020_14.pdf.

Emergency Events Database (EM-DAT). 2022. *Disasters in numbers 2021.* Brussel: EM-DAT, the International Disaster Database. https://cred.be/sites/default/files/2021_EMDAT_report.pdf.

European Commission Joint Research Center (EU JRC). 2021. *Global Energy and Climate Outlook 2021: Advancing towards climate neutrality.* https://publications.jrc.ec.europa.eu/repository/bitstream/JRC126767/JRC126767_01.pdf.

Eurasian Research Institute (ERI). 2020. *The Wolf Economy of Mongolia.* https://www.eurasian-research.org/publication/the-wolf-economy-of-mongolia/.

Euromonitor International. 2017. *Asia Pacific in 2030: The Future Demographic.* London. https://www.euromonitor.com/asia-pacific-in-2030-the-future-demographic/report.

Federated States of Micronesia. 2022. Updated Nationally Determined Contribution of the Federated States of Micronesia for the period through 2030. https://unfccc.int/sites/default/files/NDC/2022-10/Updated%20NDC%20of%20the%20MICRONESIA.pdf.

Fensom, A. 2017. *Asia to Stay World's Fastest-Growing Region through 2030. The Diplomat.* 4 December. https://thediplomat.com/2017/12/asia-to-stay-worlds-fastest-growing-region-through-2030/.

Fiji Development Bank. 2018. *Climate Financing FDB Accredited as Direct (National) Access Entity by the Green Climate Fund.* https://www.fdb.com.fj/wp-content/uploads/2018/05/FDB-Newsletter-Bulakin-Issue-23-Jan_March_website.pdf.

Food and Agriculture Organization of the United Nations (FAO). 2021. The Impact of Disasters and Crises on Agriculture and Food Security: 2021. Rome. https://www.fao.org/3/cb3673en/cb3673en.pdf.

Fouad, M. S., N. Novta, G. Preston, T. Schneider, and S. Weerathunga. 2021. *Unlocking Access to Climate Finance for Pacific Island Countries.* Washington, DC: International Monetary Fund. https://www.elibrary.imf.org/view/journals/087/2021/020/article-A001-en.xml.

Germanwatch e. V. 2021. *Global Climate Risk Index 2021.* Prepared by D. Eckstein, V. Künzel, and L. Schäfer. Bonn.

Global Economy. 2020. Mongolia: GDP share of agriculture. https://www.theglobaleconomy.com/Mongolia/share_of_agriculture.

Global Environment Facility (GEF). 2020. Progress report on the Least Developed Countries Fund and on the Special Climate Change Fund. GEF/LDCF.SCCF..29/05. Washington, DC: Global Environment. Facility. https://www.thegef.org/sites/default/files/council-meeting-documents/EN_GEF.LDCF_.SCCF_.29_05_Progress%20Report%20on%20the%20Least%20Developed%20Countries%20Fund%20and%20the%20Special%20Climate%20Change%20Fund.pdf.

———.2021. *Project Database.* https://www.thegef.org/projects-operations/database?f%5B0%5D=approval_fy%3A2020&f%5B1%5D=approval_fy%3A2021&f%5B2%5D=regional_country_list%3A140956 (accessed 17 February 2022).

Government of Bangladesh. 2021. *Bangladesh's Citizens Climate Budget Report 2020-2021.* Dhaka. https://www.bd.undp.org/content/bangladesh/en/home/library/environment_energy/climate-budget-report-bangladeshs-citizens-2020-21.html.

———. Ministry of Environment, Forest, and Climate Change (MoEFCC). 2022. National Adaptation Plan of Bangladesh (2023-2050). https://www4.unfccc.int/sites/SubmissionsStaging/Documents/202211020942---National%20Adaptation%20Plan%20of%20Bangladesh%20(2023-2050).pdf.

———. Ministry of Finance (MOF). 2018. *Climate Public Finance Tracking in Bangladesh: Approach and Methodology.* Dhaka. https://www.bd.undp.org/content/dam/bangladesh/docs/Publications/Pub-2019/Final%20Climate%20Public%20Finance%20Tracking.pdf.

———. Ministry of Power, Energy and Mineral Resources. 2021. Energy Scenario of Bangladesh 2020-21. https://www4.unfccc.int/sites/SubmissionsStaging/Documents/202211020942---National%20Adaptation%20Plan%20of%20Bangladesh%20(2023-2050).pdf.

Government of the Cook Islands. Ministry of Foreign Affairs and Immigration. 2022. National Statement by Prime Minister Hon. Mark Brown at the UNFCCC COP 27. https://mfai.gov.ck/news-updates/national-statement-prime-minister-hon-mark-brown-unfcc-cop-27.

Government of Fiji. 2019. *ECAL in Action How Your Environment and Climate Adaptation Levy is Building a Better, Stronger Fiji. Government of Fiji.* https://www.fiji.gov.fj/getattachment/e71b8d61-ce72-48fc-bca2-eeeff2d8739b/Environment-Climate-Adaptation-Levy.aspx [Accessed 18 April 2022].

———.2019. *World's First-Ever Relocation Trust Fund for People Displaced by Climate Change Launched by Fijian Prime Minister.* https://www.fiji.gov.fj/Media-Centre/News/WORLD'S-FIRST--EVER-RELOCATION-TRUST-FUND-FOR-PEOP.

———. Ministry of Economy. 2019. *Budget Estimates 2019-2020. Parliament of the Republic of Fiji,* p.318. http://www.parliament.gov.fj/wp-content/uploads/2019/06/2019-2020-budget-estimates.pdf [Accessed 18 April 2022]

Government of India. 2022. India's Updated First Nationally Determined Contribution Under Paris Agreement (2021-2030). https://unfccc.int/sites/default/files/NDC/2022-08/India%20Updated%20First%20Nationally%20Determined%20Contrib.pdf.

———. Ministry of Environment, Forest and Climate Change (MoEFCC). 2022. India's long-term low-carbon development strategy. Ministry of Environment, Forest and Climate Change, Government of India. https://unfccc.int/sites/default/files/resource/India_LTLEDS.pdf.

Government of Indonesia. 2020. *National Medium-Term Development Plan 2020-2024: Appendix–Presidential Regulation No. 18 of 2020.* https://perpustakaan.bappenas.go.id/e-library/file_upload/koleksi/migrasi-data-publikasi/file/RP_RKP/Narasi-RPJMN-2020-2024-versi-Bahasa-Inggris.pdf.

———. 2021. *Data Realisasi Pinjaman dan Hibah Luar Negeri 2012-2019 (Realization data of Foreign Loans and 2012-2019.* https://www.bappenas.go.id/datapublikasishow?q=Laporan%20Kinerja%20Pelaksanaan%20Pinjaman/Hibah%20Luar%20Negeri.

———. 2021. *Strategic Role of Various Climate Change Financing in Indonesia.* Jakarta. https://fiskal.kemenkeu.go.id/nda_gcf/en/news/strategic-role-of-various-climate-change-financing-in-indonesia.

———. Ministry of Energy and Mineral Resources (MEMR), 2021. Regulation No. 26/2021. https://ebtke.esdm.go.id/post/2022/01/21/3058/implementasi.peraturan.menteri.esdm.tentang.plts.atap.

———. Ministry of Finance (MOF). 2018. *Climate Change Financing Framework.* Kathmandu. https://mof.gov.np/uploads/document/file/CCFF_FINAL_Web_20180222050438.pdf.

———. Ministry of National Development Planning (BAPPENAS). 2019. *Hadiri Eastern Economic Forum: Menteri Bambang Paparkan Kebijakan dan Target Investasi Indonesia di 2024 (Attending Eastern Economic Forum: Minister Bambang Explains Indonesia's Investment Policy and Targets in 2024).* Jakarta. https://www.bappenas.go.id/index.php/berita/hadiri-eastern-economic-forum-menteri-bambang-paparkan-kebijakan-dan-target-investasi-indonesia-di-2024.

———. Ministry of Public Works and Public Housing. 2020. Rencana Strategis Tahun 2020–2024 (Strategic Plan Year 2020–2024). Jakarta. https://pu.go.id/assets/media/1927846278Buku%20Renstra%20Kementerian%20PUPR%202020-2024.pdf.

Government of Mongolia. 2020. *Mongolia First NDC (Updated Submission)* https://unfccc.int/sites/default/files/NDC/2022-06/First%20Submission%20of%20Mongolia%27s%20NDC.pdf.

Government of Nepal. Ministry of Federal Affairs and Local Development (MOFAGA). 2018. *District Climate Public Expenditure and Institutional Review. Kathmandu.* https://www.np.undp.org/content/nepal/en/home/library/environment_energy/district-climate-public-expenditure-and-institutional-review.html.

———. Ministry of Finance (MOF). 2018. Climate Change Financing Framework. Kathmandu. https://mof.gov.np/uploads/document/file/CCFF_FINAL_Web_20180222050438.pdf.

Government of the People's Republic of China. 2021. *China First NDC (Updated Submission).* https://cop23.unfccc.int/sites/default/files/NDC/2022-06/China%E2%80%99s%20Achievements%2C%20New%20Goals%20and%20New%20Measures%20for%20Nationally%20Determined%20Contributions.pdf.

Government of Sri Lanka. Ministry of Environment. 2021. Updated Nationally Determined Contributions. https://unfccc.int/sites/default/files/NDC/2022-06/Amendmend%20to%20the%20Updated%20Nationally%20Determined%20Contributions%20of%20Sri%20Lanka.pdf.

Government of Thailand. 2022. 2nd Updated Nationally Determined Contribution. https://unfccc.int/sites/default/files/NDC/2022-11/Thailand%202nd%20Updated%20NDC.pdf.

———. Ministry of Natural Resources and Environment. 2022. *Thailand's Long-term Low Greenhouse Gas Emission Development Strategy.* https://unfccc.int/sites/default/files/resource/Thailand%20LT-LEDS%20%28Revised%20Version%29_08Nov2022.pdf.

Government of Timor Leste. 2022. Updated Nationally Determined Contribution 2022-2030.
https://unfccc.int/sites/default/files/NDC/2022-11/Timor_Leste%20Updated%20NDC%202022_2030.pdf.

Government of Tuvalu. 2022. Updated Nationally Determined Contribution (NDC).
https://unfccc.int/sites/default/files/NDC/2023-02/Tuvalus%20Updated%20NDC%20for%20UNFCCC%20Submission.pdf.

Government of Vanuatu. 2022. Vanuatu's Revised and Enhanced 1st Nationally Determined Contribution 2021–2030.
https://unfccc.int/sites/default/files/NDC/2022-08/Vanuatu%20NDC%20Revised%20and%20Enhanced.pdf.

Green Climate Fund (GCF). *2020. Annual Portfolio Performance Report (2019).* GCF/B.27/Inf.04. Incheon.
https://www.greenclimate.fund/sites/default/files/document/gcf-b27-inf04.pdf

—————.2021. Annual Portfolio Performance Report (2020). GCF/B.30/Inf.09. Incheon.
https://www.greenclimate.fund/sites/default/files/document/gcf-b30-inf09.pdf.

Hourcade, J. C., Y. Glemarec, H. de Coninck, F. Bayat-Renoux, K. Ramakrishna, and A. Revi. 2021. *Scaling Up Climate Finance in the Context of COVID-19.* Republic of Korea: Green Climate Fund.
https://www.greenclimate.fund/sites/default/files/document/
scaling-climate-finance-context-covid-19-executive-summary_0.pdf.

Hutfilter, U. F., A. Zimmer, F. Saeed, B. Hare, T. Aboumahboub, I. Kelischek, C.F. Schleussner, P. Y. Parra, A. Ancygier, R. Brecha, J. Granadillos, G. Ganti, R. Vyas, and M. Schaeffer. 2019. *Decarbonising South and South East Asia.* New York: Climate Analytics.
https://climateanalytics.org/media/decarbonisingasia2019-fullreport-climateanalytics.pdf.

Indonesia Climate Change Trust Fund (ICCTF). 2020. *ICCTF Annual Report 2020.*
https://www.icctf.or.id/portfolio-item/annual-report-icctf-2020/.

Institute for Essential Services Reform (IESR). 2021. *Indonesia Energy Transition Outlook 2021: Tracking Progress of Energy Transition in Indonesia.* Report prepared by A. P. Tampubolon, D. Kurniawan, D. Arinaldo, I. Marciano, J. Christian, P. Simamora, and H. Prasojo. Jakarta.
https://iesr.or.id/en/pustaka/indonesia-energy-transition-outlook-ieto-2021.

Intergovernmental Panel on Climate Change (IPCC). 2022. *Climate Change 2022: Impacts, Adaptation, and Vulnerability.* Contribution of Working Group II to the Sixth Assessment Report of the IPCC. H. O. Pörtner, D. C. Roberts, M. Tignor, E. S. Poloczanska, K. Mintenbeck, A. Alegria, M. Craig, S. Langsdorf, S. Löschke, V. Möller, A. Okem, and B. Rama, eds. Geneva. https://www.ipcc.ch/report/sixth-assessment-report-working-group-ii/.

International Climate Initiative (IKI). 2019. *Mongolia: Taking Climate Action seriously.*
https://www.international-climate-initiative.com/en/iki-media/news/mongolia_taking_climate_action_seriously/.

International Council on Clean Transportation (ICCT). 2021. *Race to Zero: How Manufacturers are Positioned for Zero-Emission Commercial Trucks and Buses in China.* Prepared by S. Mao and F. Rodriguez.
https://theicct.org/wp-content/uploads/2021/12/china-race-to-zero-aug2021.pdf.

International Energy Agency (IEA). 2020. *World Energy Outlook 2020.* Paris.
https://www.iea.org/reports/world-energy-outlook-2020.

International Federation of Red Cross and Red Crescent Societies (IFRC). 2022. Philippines: Typhoon Rai (Odette).
https://www.ifrc.org/press-release/philippines-new-data-reveals-typhoon-rai-wrecked-15-million-houses-0.

International Finance Corporation (IFC). 2017. *Climate Investment Opportunities in South Asia - An IFC Analysis.* https://www.ifc.org/wps/wcm/connect/topics_ext_content/ifc_external_corporate_site/climate+business/resources/final+climate+investment+opportunities+in+south+asia+-+an+ifc+analysis.

————.2019. Global Progress Report of the Sustainable Banking Network. Washington, DC. https://www.ifc.org/wps/wcm/connect/topics_ext_content/ifc_external_corporate_site/sustainability-at-ifc/company-resources/sustainable-finance/sbn_2019+globalprogressreport.

International Monetary Fund (IMF). 2021a. IMF Executive Directors Discuss a New SDR Allocation of US$650 billion to Boost Reserves, Help Global Recovery from COVID-19. Press Release No. 21/ 77. 23 March. http://www.imf.org/en/News/Articles/2021/03/23/pr2177-imf-execdir-discuss-newsdrallocation-us-650b-boost-reserves-help-global-recovery-covid19.

————.2021b. *Unlocking Access to Climate Finance for Pacific Island Countries.* Departmental paper prepared by M. Fouad, N. Novta, G. Preston, T. Schneider, and S. Weerathunga. Washington, DC. https://www.imf.org/en/Publications/Departmental-Papers-Policy-Papers/Issues/2021/09/23/Unlocking-Access-to-Climate-Finance-for-Pacific-Islands-Countries-464709.

IMF Climate Change Dashboard. 2022. *Climate Change Indicators Dashboard: A statistical tool linking climate considerations and global economic indicators.* https://climatedata.imf.org/.

International Renewable Energy Agency (IRENA). 2019a. Renewable Energy Statistics 2019. Abu Dhabi. https://www.irena.org/publications/2019/Jul/Renewable-energy-statistics-2019.

————.2019b. Renewable Power Generation Costs in 2018. Abu Dhabi. https://www.irena.org/publications/2019/May/Renewable-power-generation-costs-in-2018.

————.2020. Renewable Energy Statistics 2020. Abu Dhabi. https://www.irena.org/-/media/Files/IRENA/Agency/Publication/2020/Jul/IRENA_Renewable_Energy_Statistics_2020.pdf?rev=3a5e14b11fe6434dbc3e59b7bbacd6e7.

Jang, D. 2021. *The World Can't Fight Climate Change Without East Asia on Board.* The Diplomat. 23 April. Washington, DC. https://thediplomat.com/2021/04/the-world-cant-fight-climate-change-without-east-asia-on-board/.

Klein RJT, Huq S, Denton F, Downing T.E. et al. 2007. *"Inter-relationships between Adaptation and Mitigation."* Climate Change 2007: Impacts, Adaptation and Vulnerability. Contribution of Working Group II to the Fourth Assessment Report of the Intergovernmental Panel on Climate Change. M.L. Parry, O.F. Canziani, J.P. Palutikof, P.J. van der Linden and C.E. Hanson, (eds.,) Cambridge University Press, Cambridge, UK, pp 745 -777.

Kulp, S.A. and Strauss, B. H. 2019. *New elevation data triple estimates of global vulnerability to sea-level rise and coastal flooding.* Nat Commun 10, 4844 (2019). https://doi.org/10.1038/s41467-019-12808-z.

Maclellan, N. and Meads, S. 2016. After Paris: Climate finance in the Pacific islands Strengthening collaboration, accelerating access and prioritising adaptation for vulnerable communities. Australia: Oxfam Research Report. https://www.oxfam.org.au/wp-content/uploads/2016/09/FULL-REPORT-text-only-After-Paris-Climate-Finance-in-the-Pacific.pdf.

Martinus, M., and Q. Jiahui. 2022. Climate Finance in Southeast Asia: Trends and Opportunities. *ISEAS Perspective.* 9 February. Singapore: ISEAS–Yusof Ishak Institute. https://fulcrum.sg/climate-finance-in-southeast-asia-trends-and-opportunities/.

Meattle, C., and M. Zeki. 2020. Uncovering the Private Climate Finance Landscape in Indonesia. 15 May. San Francisco: Climate Policy Initiative. https://www.climatepolicyinitiative.org/uncovering-the-private-climate-finance-landscape-in-indonesia/.

Mongolia Sustainable Finance Association (MSFA). 2019. *Mongolia Green Taxonomy.* https://www.ifc.org/wps/wcm/connect/0c296cd3-be1e-4e2f-a6cb-f507ad7bdfe9/Mongolia+Green+Taxanomy+ENG+PDF+for+publishing.pdf?MOD=AJPERES&CVID=nikyhlh.

Oliver, P., A. Clark, and A. Falconer. 2019. *Measuring the Private Capital Response to Climate Change: A Proposed Dashboard. CPI Climate Finance Tracking Brief.* San Francisco: Climate Policy Initiative. https://climatepolicyinitiative.org/publication/measuring-the-private-capital-response-to-climate-change-a-proposed-dashboard/.

Organisation for Economic Co-operation and Development (OECD). 2021. Developed Countries Likely to Reach USD 100 Billion Goal in 2023. Statement by the OECD Secretary-General on Future Levels of Climate Finance. 25 October. https://www.oecd.org/newsroom/statement-by-the-oecd-secretary-general-on-future-levels-of-climate-finance.htm.

————.2022. Focus on Green Recovery. https://www.oecd.org/coronavirus/en/themes/green-recovery (accessed 29 April 2022).

Partnerships in Environmental Management for the Seas of East Asia (PEMSEA). 2015. *SDS-SEA: Sustainable Development Strategy of the Seas of East Asia.* http://www.pemsea.org/sites/default/files/SDS-SEA%202015%20FINAL%2011272015%20FULL%20rev_1.pdf.

Potsdam Institute for Climate Impact Research and Climate Analytics (PIK). 2013. *Turn Down the Heat: Climate Extremes, Regional Impacts, and the Case for Resilience.* Washington, DC: World Bank. https://openknowledge.worldbank.org/handle/10986/14000.

PT Sarana Multi Infrastruktur (PT SMI). 2020. *Annual Report PT SMI 2020.* https://ptsmi.co.id/cfind/source/files/annual-report/annual-report-pt-smi-2020.pdf.

Republic of Indonesia. 2022. Enhanced Nationally Determined Contribution. https://unfccc.int/sites/default/files/NDC/2022-09/ENDC%20Indonesia.pdf.

Republic of Kiribati. 2022. Nationally Determined Contribution (Revised). https://unfccc.int/sites/default/files/NDC/2023-03/221213%20Kiribati%20NDC%20Web%20Quality.pdf.

Republic of the Philippines. 2021. Republic of the Philippines Nationally Determined Contribution. https://unfccc.int/sites/default/files/NDC/2022-06/Philippines%20-%20NDC.

Republic of Uzbekistan. 2017. Intended Nationally Determined Contributions. https://unfccc.int/sites/default/files/NDC/2022-06/INDC%20Uzbekistan%2018-04-2017_Eng.pdf.

————.2021. Updated Nationally Determined Contribution. https://unfccc.int/sites/default/files/NDC/2022-06/Uzbekistan_Updated%20NDC_2021_EN.pdf.

Reuters. 2020. China's Greenhouse Emissions Rise 2.6% in 2019: Research Group. 18 March. https://www.reuters.com/article/us-china-environment-carbon-emission-idUSKBN2150YY.

Richmond, M., and K. Hallmeyer. 2019. Tracking Adaptation Finance: Advancing Methods to Capture Finance Flows in the Landscape. San Francisco: Climate Policy Initiative. https://www.climatepolicyinitiative.org/wp-content/uploads/2019/12/Tracking-Adaptation-Finance-Brief.pdf.

Rhodium Group. 2021. China's Greenhouse Gas Emissions Exceeded the Developed World for the First Time in 2019. Prepared by K. Larsen, H. Pitt, M. Grant, and T. Houser. https://rhg.com/research/chinas-emissions-surpass-developed-countries/.

Samuwai, J. 2021. Understanding the Climate Finance Landscape and How to Scale It Up in Pacific Small Island Developing States. United Nations ESCAP, Macroeconomic Policy and Financing for Development Division, September 2021. Bangkok. https://www.unescap.org/sites/default/d8files/knowledge-products/Working%20Paper_Climate%20finance_PSIDS_final.pdf.

Samuwai, J. and Hills, J.M. 2018. Assessing Climate Finance Readiness in the Asia-Pacific Region. https://www.researchgate.net/publication/324536740_Assessing_Climate_Finance_Readiness_in_the_Asia-Pacific_Region.

Schleussner, C., Lissner, T. K., Fischer, E. M., Wohland, J., Perrette, M., Golly, A., Rogelj, J., Childers, K., Schewe, J., Frieler, K., Mengel, M., Hare, W., and Schaeffer, M. 2016. Differential climate impacts for policy-relevant limits to global warming: the case of 1.5 °C and 2 °C. Germany: Earth System Dynamic. https://esd.copernicus.org/articles/7/327/2016/esd-7-327-2016.pdf.

Secretariat of Pacific Regional Environment Programme (SPREP). 2019. Sea Level Rise Washing Over Maritime Boundaries In the Pacific. https://www.sprep.org/news/sea-level-rise-washing-over-maritime-boundaries-in-the-pacific.

Statista. 2022. Carbon Dioxide Emissions from Energy Worldwide from 1965 to 2021, by Region. New York. https://www.statista.com/statistics/2059 66/world-carbon-dioxide-emissions-by-region/#:~:text=The%20Asia%2DPacific%20region%20produced,percent%20o f%20the%20global%20total.

Stenek, V., J.-C. Amado, and D. Greenall. 2013. Enabling Environment for Private Sector Adaptation: An Index Assessment Framework. Washington, DC: International Finance Corporation. http://documents.worldbank.org/curated/en/734691487221282291/Enabling-environment-forprivate-sector-adaptation-an-index-assessment-framework.

Sumner, A., C. Hoy, and E. Ortiz-Juarez. 2020. Estimates of the Impact of COVID-19 on Global Poverty. WIDER Working Paper No. 43/ 2020. Helsinki: United Nations University–World Institute for Development Economic Research (UNU-WIDER).

Swart, R., and F. Raes. 2007. Making Integration of Adaptation and Mitigation Work: Mainstreaming into Sustainable Development Policies? Climate Policy. 7 (4). pp. 288–303.

Swiss Re Institute. 2021. The Economics of Climate Change: No Action Not an Option. Zurich. https://www.swissre.com/dam/jcr:e73ee7c3-7f83-4c17-a2b8-8ef23a8d3312/swiss-re-institute-expertise-publication-economics-of-climate-change.pdf.

Tao, Z., and L. Han. 2022. Emergency Response, Influence and Lessons in the 2021 Compound Disaster in Henan Province of China. International Journal of Environmental Research and Public Health. 19 (1). 488. https://doi.org/10.3390/ijerph19010488.

United Nations Department of Economic and Social Affairs, Population Division. 2022. World Population Prospects 2022. https://population.un.org/wpp/.

United Nations Development Programme (UNDP). 2018. Climate Public Finance Tracking in Bangladesh: Approach and Methodology. https://www.bd.undp.org/content/dam/bangladesh/docs/Publications/Pub-2019/Final%20Climate%20Public%20Finance%20Tracking.pdf.

————.2021a. *Budgeting for Climate Change: A Guidance Note for Governments to Integrate Climate Change into Budgeting*. New York. https://www.undp.org/sites/g/files/zskgke326/files/2021-10/UNDP-RBAP-Budgeting-for-Climate-Change-Guidance-Note-2021.pdf.

————.2021b. *Mongolian SDG Finance Taxonomy Development discussed at 2021 GFLP Webinar on Sustainable Finance*. Mongolia. https://www.undp.org/mongolia/press-releases/mongolian-sdg-finance-taxonomy-development-discussed-2021-gflp-webinar-sustainable-finance.

United Nations Economic and Social Commission for Asia and the Pacific (UNESCAP). 2016. *The Economics of Climate Change in the Asia-Pacific Region*. Bangkok. https://www.unescap.org/sites/default/files/The%20Economics%20of%20Climate%20Change%20%20in%20the%20Asia-Pacific%20region.pdf.

————.2021. Asia-Pacific Disaster Report 2021: *Resilience in a Riskier World*. Bangkok. https://www.unescap.org/sites/default/d8files/knowledge-products/Asia-Pacific%20Disaster%20Report%202021_full%20version_0.pdf.

UNESCAP, UNEP, UN Women, and greenwerk. 2021. *Is 1.5°C within Reach for the Asia-Pacific Region?* Thailand. https://www.unescap.org/sites/default/d8files/knowledge-products/Assessment%20of%20AP%20Climate%20Ambition_Final_update.pdf.

United Nations Environment Programme (UNEP). 2016. Definitions and Concepts: Background Note. *Inquiring Working Paper*. 16/13. September. Nairobi. http://unepinquiry.org/wp-content/uploads/2016/09/1_Definitions_and_Concepts.pdf.

————.2020. *Emissions Gap Report 2020*. Nairobi. https://www.unep.org/emissions-gap-report-2020.

————.2021. *Adaptation Gap Report 2020*. Prepared in association with the UNEP DTU Partnership and the World Adaptation Science Programme (WASP). Nairobi. https://www.unep.org/resources/adaptation-gap-report-2020.

————.2021. *Emissions Gap Report 2021: The Heat Is On – A World of Climate Promises Not Yet Delivered*. Nairobi. https://www.unep.org/resources/emissions-gap-report-2021?gclid=Cj0KCQjw4NujBhC5ARIsAF4Iv6djr_SWINdZcTaSYNMP4KbWSZLk5t27lnHN8-7wLN9H4Sc2Lr4k4m4aAjgKEALw_wcB.

United Nations Framework Convention on Climate Change (UNFCCC). 2018. *2018 Biennial Assessment and Overview of Climate Finance Flows: Technical Report*. Prepared by the Standing Committee on Finance. Bonn. https://unfccc.int/sites/default/files/resource/2018%20BA%20Technical%20Report%20Final%20Feb%202019.pdf.

————.2021. *Emissions Gap Report 2021: The Heat Is On – A World of Climate Promises Not Yet Delivered*. Nairobi. 2021. COP26 Reaches Consensus on Key Actions to Address Climate Change. UN Climate Press Release. 13 Nov. https://unfccc.int/news/cop26-reaches-consensus-on-key-actions-to-address-climate-change.

United Nations Office for Disaster Risk Reduction (UNDDR). 2022. The Central Asia Initiative of the European Union during the COVID-19 Crisis: The Way Forward in Preparing for and Managing Risks. Geneva. https://reliefweb.int/report/kazakhstan/central-asia-initiative-european-union-during-covid-19-crisis-way-forward.

Vivid Economics and Finance for Biodiversity Initiative. 2021. Greenness of Stimulus Index: An Assessment of COVID-19 Stimulus by G20 Countries and Other Major Economies in Relation to Climate Action and Biodiversity Goals. London. https://www.vivideconomics.com/wp-content/uploads/2021/07/Green-Stimulus-Index-6th-Edition_final-report.pdf.

Wahid, M. n.d. Net-Metering Reference Guide for Electricity Consumer. Alternative Energy Development Board, Ministry of Water and Power. Pakistan. https://www.aedb.org/images/NetmeteringGuidlinesforConsumers.pdf.

World Bank. 2010. Economics of Adaptation to Climate Change: Bangladesh. Washington, DC. https://openknowledge.worldbank.org/bitstream/handle/10986/12837/702660v10ESW0P0IC000EACC0Bangladesh.pdf?sequence=1&isAllowed=y.

———.2020. Financing Climate Actions in Central Asia: A Survey of International and Local Investments. Study commissioned by the Regional Environmental Centre for Central Asia (CAREC) under the Climate Adaptation and Mitigation Programme for the Aral Sea Basin (CAMP4ASB). Washington, DC. https://zoinet.org/wp-content/uploads/2020/10/CA-climate-finance-en.pdf.

———.2021. Climate Change Action Plan 2021–2025 South Asia Roadmap. https://openknowledge.worldbank.org/bitstream/handle/10986/36321/164599.pdf.

———.2022. South Asia Climate Roadmap. https://www.worldbank.org/en/region/sar/publication/south-asia-climate-roadmap.

World Bank Group (WBG) and Asian Development Bank (ADB). 2021e. *Climate Risk Country Profile: Indonesia.* Washington, DC. https://climateknowledgeportal.worldbank.org/sites/default/files/2021-05/15504-Indonesia%20Country%20Profile-WEB_0.pdf.

World Meteorological Organization (WMO). 2016. Tropical cyclone operational plan for the South Pacific and South-East Indian Ocean. p.74. https://www.wmo.int/pages/prog/www/tcp/documents/RAV_OpPlan_TCP-24_WMO-1181_2016_Final.pdf.

www.ingramcontent.com/pod-product-compliance
Lightning Source LLC
Chambersburg PA
CBHW050046220326
41599CB00045B/7299